T0208143

Disability and Dependency

Disability, Handicap and Life Chances
Series Editor: Len Barton

Disability and Dependency

Edited by
Len Barton
Bristol Polytechnic

Routledge
Taylor & Francis Group
LONDON AND NEW YORK

First published in 1989 RoutledgeFalmer

Published 2021 by Routledge
2 Park Square, Milton Park, Abingdon, Oxon OX14 4RN
605 Third Avenue, New York, NY 10017

*Routledge is an imprint of the Taylor & Francis Group, an
informa business*

British Library Cataloguing in Publication Data

Disability and Dependency
   1. Physically handicapped Persons. Social adjustment
   I. Barton, Len
   362.4
   ISBN 13: 978-1-85000-616-9 (hbk)
   ISBN 13: 978-1-85000-617-6 (pbk)

Typeset in 10½/13 Bembo by
Input Typesetting Ltd, London

Contents

To Rachel and Sarai

Preface

The revised papers in this volume were first presented at an International Conference on Disability, Handicap and Policy at Bristol Polytechnic, England in July 1988.

The intention behind the Conference was to provide a forum in which perspectives, research findings, and policy developments could be presented to critical scrutiny. This it was hoped would lead to a strengthening of our commitment to the empowerment of disabled people.

Speakers and delegates came from many different countries.

Grateful thanks are due to Falmer Press, to Christine Cox, Sarah King and Malcolm Clarkson for their important support and encouragement in the planning and running of the Conference.

Thanks are also due to the British Council for offering some financial support for the Conference.

Acknowledgement

I am grateful to Christine Cox for her advice and encouragement that enabled this book to be published.
Len Barton, 1989

Introduction

Len Barton

Understanding the issue of disability is a difficult task in that the factors involved are complex and contentious. They are complex because they entail the intermeshing of social, political and economic factors and are contentious in that the parties involved are motivated by different ideological concerns and objectives. Particular groups have been instrumental in establishing forms of discourse that have legitimated specific images and explanations. These have contributed to the generation of various policies and practices. All views are not of equal significance or value as can be seen from the dominance of professional discourse in the field of disability, particularly that derived from medicine and psychology. The outcome of this has been a form of reductionism in which problems are individualised and the necessity and centrality of professional judgement and practice has been powerfully legitimated. (See Ryan *et al*, 1980; Scull, 1979; Tomlinson, 1982; Ford *et al*, 1982).

Disabled people have become increasingly critical of the role of professionals in their lives, in that such encounters have been viewed as essentially demeaning and oppressive. Part of their criticism is that they have a voice but it is not being listened to, and that their perspective is under-valued. The concerns they raise are fundamental and include the extent to which they control their own bodies and lives. They demand the opportunity to make decisions and exercise choices, and thus the question of empowerment is central to their objectives (see Oliver, 1986; Abberley, 1987; Brisenden, 1986).

The chapters in this volume support such critiques and endeavours, and provide a series of indictments with regard to the ways in which policies and practices in particular countries have been generated and implemented. It is not merely a question of the disjunctions between policy and practice, the inappropriateness of specific provisions or the contradictory nature of others. The heart of the condemnation is that disabled people have been subject to modes of socialisation, particularly with professionals, which have been fundamentally disabling. They constantly experience encounters with significant others which create dependency and helplessness.

In the opening chapter Oliver examines the ways in which welfare systems have created whole classes of people who have become dependent upon the State for many aspects of their lives. He places the question of disability within the general inequalities and disadvantages of contemporary industrial societies. Thus disabled people are different in degree to other oppressed groups. He argues that dependency is not the result of functional limitations of disabled people. Indeed, he contends that by concentrating on the latter, various offensive images of disability have been legitimated. These include those which depict disability in personal tragedy or heroic terms. Part of the struggle is to critique such perspectives and replace them with one which highlights the significance of economic and political processes, and of professional judgment and practices in the production of dependency.

The idea that human services are concerned with positive, humane and enriching practices and relationships is seriously challenged by Wolfensberger. Whilst all such services have stated purposes, or 'manifest functions', it is the 'latent functions' which are often the most powerful. These are the unacknowledged functions of human services which are achieved in subtle and indirect ways. He maintains that in a post-primary production economy in which human services have become increasingly important, the human service sector creates and sustains large numbers of dependent people. In such societies dependent and devalued people are needed in order to provide employment for others. The real intent of society is thus hidden.

Whatever designs a government or state may have with regard to various social policies, it is essential to recognise that their implementation is always through human agency. By using Lipsky's theory of 'street-level bureaucracy' as an analytical tool of explanation, Hudson in his chapter considers that group of workers who are at the sharp-end of human service activity. He maintains that in order to understand how and why organisations often function in contradiction to any stated intentions, we have to appreciate how key personnel experience particular work contexts. This includes the discretion they have, the pressures they encounter and the strategies they develop in order to survive. The analysis of these processes and relationships must be informed by an understanding of the structural conditions of welfare institutions within the broader foundations of a given society. Thus, he is able to contend that the poorer people are, the greater the extent of control street-level bureaucrats will exercise over their lives.

The fundamental issue for Abberley is that disabled people are oppressed. He is critical of false and offensive explanations of the origin and nature of those differences between the lives of disabled and non-disabled people. The danger of social stereotyping is recognised and the issue of the power of definitions of normality, particularly those of the medical and welfare professions, are discussed. Those models of disabled people as 'really' normal are viewed as profoundly mistaken and a means of perpetuating the oppression of disabled people. By examining the inadequacy of Social Work Education and particular types of empathetic identification within such training programmes, alongside a consideration of recent legislative changes, he argues that disabled people will experience more economic and psychological suffering and this will make independence less likely to be realised.

Supporting many of the ideas already outlined, Candappa and Burgess reinforce the importance of investigating how particular groups of disabled people experience the social world, including how they are treated by various professionals. Reporting on a participant observation study within a hospital setting, the authors discuss the life conditions of a group of people with a mental handicap, the perspectives and practice of their carers and the impact these have on the self images of their subjects of study. A concern of the study was with the extent to which the nurses understood and accepted the normalisation principle. In some vivid examples the authors are able to highlight the continued dominance of negative evaluations and essentially custodial practices within the daily routine of hospital life. Insightful incidents are recorded which begin to demonstrate the ways in which the residents within the hospital are socialised into passive roles.

The remaining three chapters illustrate the importance of comparative insights into policy and practice and provide some valuable information and understanding of developments within other societies.

In their chapter Blythman and Spivack discuss some of their research into a programme which attempts to meet the special needs of multi-risk families in Brooklyn, New York City. Their case study is set within a more general analysis of the enormous and growing disparity in the States between the rich and the poor. Whilst the rhetoric of the 'American Dream' is constantly articulated in various forms through the media, the harsh reality for many groups, including disabled people, is one of hardship, poverty and disadvantage. This includes having to deal with public agencies that are user-unfriendly, bureaucratic, repressing and disabling.

Developing rehabilitation policies and services in South West Asia is the subject of the chapter by Miles. In his discussion he notes that formulated disability policy is a recent notion, and that developing a policy through public participation of specific targeted groups is an activity with which Asian governments are unfamiliar. Historically, society has been seen to have few rights over individuals who are disabled. The support and care required has been the responsibility of the family. Stigmatising attitudes are analysed within the context of economic and cultural differences and the inappropriateness of Western advice. Through time, conflicts have developed between what Governments wanted to do and were advised to do, and what they attempted to do and what actually happened. Too often, Miles argues, there is an unacceptable gulf between a Government identifying a problem and practical stages being taken to deal with the issue.

The final chapter by Jones and Pullen is an account of some key findings from a research project they have been undertaking in several European countries. The research was concerned with the importance of understanding deaf people and trying to ascertain their views on a range of policies and practices relating to education and training, employment and health. In many instances deaf people experienced inadequate support in terms of interpreters, were offered inappropriate materials, provided with limited opportunities and too often were underemployed. One of the fundamental insights drawn from this research is that deaf people experience a great deal of isolationism and are largely excluded from the key decision-making processes about their own lives.

Although the contributors to this volume do not share a single unified perspective, their chapters do highlight some common concerns. These include the conviction that:

> Too often there is an unacceptable disjuncture between the public rhetoric of representatives of governments or institutions and actual practices or outcomes.
>
> Human service industries and the professional practices involved are fundamentally disabling.
>
> The question of rights is central to the whole issue of disability.
>
> Demands for a greater empowerment of disabled people are essential.
>
> Disabled people need to be listened to and involved in key decision-making.

Achieving these objectives and establishing more informed perspectives necessitates a difficult struggle.

One of the disturbing messages that this book offers is the extent to which, within the socio-economic arrangements and relations of a given society, disabled people are suffering. This includes the economic, material and personal aspects of their lives.

Various contributors offer ways of combating the discriminating relations and practices which disabled people experience. A crucial requirement is the recognition of the politics of disability and the urgency for disabled people to organise themselves more collectively and effectively. They must struggle to make themselves heard through as many avenues as possible. This will include strengthening their belief in the importance of their perspectives. Able-bodied people should be encouraged to help in this campaign.

Hopefully, this book will make some small contribution to keeping the debates alive and provide valuable ideas to inform the struggle for greater independence on the part of disabled people.

References

Abberley, P. (1987) 'The Concept of Oppression and the Development of a Social Theory of Disability', *Disability, Handicap and Society*, 2, 1, pp. 5–20.

Brisenden, S. (1986) 'Independent Living and the Medical Model of Disability', *Disability, Handicap and Society*, 1, 2, pp. 173–178.

Ford, J., Mongon, D. and Whelan, M. (1982) *Special Education and Social Control*, London, Routledge & Kegan Paul.

Oliver, M. (1986) 'Social Policy and Disability: Some Theoretical Issues', *Disability, Handicap and Society*, 1, 1, pp. 5–18.

Ryan, J. and Thomas, F. (1980) *The Politics of Mental Handicap*, Harmondsworth, Penguin.

Scull, A. T. (1979) *Museums of Madness: The Social Organisation of Insanity in Nineteenth-Century England*, London, Allen Lane.

Tomlinson, S. (1982) *The Sociology of Special Education*, London, Routledge & Kegan Paul.

Chapter One

Disability and Dependency: A Creation of Industrial Societies?

Mike Oliver

The Social Construction of the Disability Problem

The category disability is not fixed and absolute, but can be, and indeed has been, defined in a variety of different ways throughout history, within particular societies and in any given social context. The fact that definitions of disability are relative rather than absolute have led some sociologists in particular to conclude that disability can only be properly understood as a social construction.

> We contend that disability definitions are not rationally determined but socially constructed. Despite the objective reality, what becomes a disability is determined by the social meanings individuals attach to particular physical and mental impairments. Certain disabilities become defined as social problems through the successful efforts of powerful groups to market their own self interests. Consequently the so-called 'objective' criteria of disability reflects the biases, self-interests, and moral evaluations of those in a position to influence policy.
>
> (Albrecht and Levy, 1981, 14)

But this process of social construction is not dependent solely on individual meanings or the activities of powerful groups and vested interests, for the category disability is itself produced in part by policy responses to it. Thus, to take an extreme position:

> Fundamentally, disability is defined by public policy. In other words, disability is whatever policy says it is. . . . The fact that disability is basically determined by public policy, moreover, seems

to demonstrate the need for careful investigations of definitions that are embedded in existing policies.

(Hahn, 1985, 294)

While not denying that policy definitions play an important role in the social construction of disability, it is clear that these definitions are themselves socially constructed. And further, it is ideology which has influenced this social construction to the point where disability has become a problem of individual disadvantage to be remedied through the development of appropriate social policies (Oliver, 1986; Borsay, 1986).

Social policy analysis has been slow to recognise the role of ideology in the development of social policies (George and Wilding, 1972) although in recent years it has been given a much more central focus (e.g. Wilding, 1982; Manning, 1985). However, disability policy has not been subjected to any rigorous analysis of its ideological underpinnings in the same way that many other social problems have been de-constructed and even re-constructed.

Although little conscious attention has been devoted to the problem, the recognition that public policy contains some unspoken assumptions about the level of physical or other abilities required to sustain a person's life seems almost inescapable.

(Hahn, 1985, 296)

There are a number of reasons why these unspoken assumptions or ideologies have not received much attention. Historically, disability policies have not developed in their own right, and so:

What is coming to be called disability policy is in fact an aggregate of a variety of policies, each with quite different origins and purposes, reflecting a historical situation in which concern for disability has been intertwined with efforts to establish policy in much broader issue area.

(Erlanger and Roth, 1985, 320)

But this is no longer true in many industrial countries which have begun to develop policies specifically in respect of disabled people. Hence the explanation for the current failure to examine these hidden assumptions or ideologies underpinning even these specific policy initiatives must lie elsewhere. Part of the answer is undoubtedly that these ideologies are so deeply embedded in social consciousness generally that they become 'facts'; they are naturalised. Thus everyone knows that disability is a personal tragedy for individuals so 'afflicted'; hence ideology becomes

7

common sense. And this common sense is reinforced both by 'aesthetic' and 'existential' anxiety:

> . . . widespread aversion toward disabled individuals may be the product of both an 'aesthetic' anxiety, which narcissistically rejects marked deviations from 'normal' physical appearances, and of an 'existential' anxiety, which may find an implicit or projected danger of dehabilitating disability even more terrifying than the inevitability of death.

> (Hahn, 1986, 125)

The central idea underpinning the social construction of disability as a particular kind of social problem has been that of dependency, and in this chapter I shall suggest that the creation of dependency amongst disabled people is an inevitable consequence of the social policies that prevail in all modern industrial societies. There are, of course, some differences of emphasis in the policies adopted towards disabled people between individual countries, but the economic, political, social, technological and ideological forces which shape these policies are sufficiently universal to make generalisations possible. It is the idea of dependency which will give a coherence to the argument to be presented and which will make generalisations possible.

The Idea of Dependency

Before considering the ways in which dependency is created, it is necessary to define what is meant by the term. In common-sense usage, dependency implies the inability to do things for oneself and consequently the reliance upon others to carry out some or all of the tasks of everyday life. Conversely, independence suggests that the individual needs no assistance whatever from anyone else and this fits nicely with the current ideological climate which stresses competitive individualism. In reality, of course, no-one in a modern industrial society is completely independent for we live in a state of mutual interdependence. The dependence of disabled people, therefore, is not a feature which marks them out as different in kind from the rest of the population but as different in degree.

There is obviously a link between this common-sense usage of the term dependency and the way it is used in discussions of social policy, but these more technical discussions see at least two dimensions to the term. The first of these concerns the ways in which welfare states have created whole groups or classes of people who become dependent upon the state for education, health care, financial support, and indeed any other provision the state is prepared to offer. The second focuses on the inability of individuals or groups to provide their own self-care because of their functional limitations or impairments. Both of these dimensions of dependency have figured large in current attempts to restructure welfare states by reducing the size and scope of state benefits and services and by shifting existing provision away from institutions and into the community.

These two dimensions have facilitated the development of reductionist explanations of the phenomenon of dependency. Psychological reductionism has focused upon the way the self-reliance of individuals and families has been eroded by the 'nanny state' and has thereby created 'pathological individuals'. Sociological reductionism has focused upon the common characteristics of different groups, of which dependency is a major feature, thereby creating 'pathological groups'. Social science has sometimes been actively involved in the creation of these reductionist explanations and the pathologising of the idea of dependency, but has also adopted a critical role in challenging them. Unfortunately, however, these challenges have had little success in influencing or shaping social policies which remain locked into the notion of dependency as pathology.

This is partly a function of the marginal role that social science plays in policy formulation, but more importantly the fact that dependency is created by a range of economic, political and professional forces beyond its influence or control. It is these matters which must now be considered. The ways in which these forces create dependency will be discussed in the context of British social policy and the services provided to disabled people by the British welfare state. There are clearly differences between welfare states in terms of their specific provisions for disabled people but all are shaped by these forces. Therefore generalisations are possible, and the implications of the analysis that follows are relevant to all industrial societies.

An Economic Basis for the Creation of Dependency

Work is central to industrial societies not simply because it produces the goods to sustain life but also because it creates particular forms of social relations. Thus anyone unable to work, for whatever reason, is likely to experience difficulties both in acquiring the necessities to sustain life physically, and also in establishing a set of satisfactory social relationships. Disabled people have not always been excluded from working but the arrival of industrial society has created particular problems:

> The speed of factory work, the enforced discipline, the time-keeping and production norms – all these were a highly unfavour-

able change from the slower, more self-determined methods of
work into which many handicapped people have been integrated.
(Ryan and Thomas, 1980, 101)

The onset of industrial society did not simply change ways of working,
but also had a profound effect on social relations with the creation of the
industrial proletariat and the gradual erosion of existing communities.
Industrialisation had profound consequences for disabled people, therefore, both in that they were less able to participate in the work process
and also because many previously acceptable social roles, such as beggar
or 'village idiot' were disappearing.

The new mechanism for controlling economically unproductive people
was the workhouse or the asylum, and over the years a whole range a
specialised institutions grew up to contain this group. These establishments were undoubtedly successful in controlling individuals who would
not or could not work. They also performed a particular ideological
function, standing as visible monuments to the fate of others who might
no longer choose to subjugate themselves to the disciplinary requirements
of the new work system. There were problems too, in that it was soon
recognised that these institutions not only created dependency in individuals but also created dependent groups. This led to fears about the 'burdens
of pauperism' in the early twentieth century, and the establishment of
Poor Law Commission. Similar concerns are around today, although, of
course, the language is different, and current moves towards community
care have a strong economic rationality underpinning them.

The point about this brief historical detour is that the issues are still the
same; disabled people are likely to face exclusion from the workforce
because of their perceived inabilities, and hence dependency is still being
created. And even where attempts are made to influence the work system,
they do not have the desired effect:

> Programs focusing on labor supply will always be a major part of
> any comprehensive approach to disability. But these efforts alone
> tend to segregate disabled people from society rather than integrate
> them into it. The alternative, or more properly the supplement, to
> these programs is a focus on the demand side of the market, making
> people more employable and more a part of general social life by
> changing the social organisation of work and of other aspects of
> everyday life, through removal of architectural barriers, nondiscri-
> miantion and affirmative action programs, mainstreaming in the
> schools, and so on. Until recently, there has been almost no concern
> with these possibilities.
>
> (Erlanger and Roth, 1985, 339)

It could, of course, be argued that government policy aimed at providing aids to employment and the adaptation of workplaces uses precisely this approach, but it does nothing of the kind. These initiatives are all geared towards the supply side of labour, at making individual disabled people more economically productive and hence more acceptable to employers. There are no government incentives to create barrier-free work environments, nor can Ford claim a grant if it wants to make its assembly line usable by all the potential workforce. Neither can other manufacturers wishing to design machinery or tools that are usable by everyone, regardless of their functional abilities, seek government assistance. There are virtually no attempts in modern industrial societies that are targeted at the social organisations of work, at the demand side of labour. And given the size of the reserve pool of labour that currently exists in most industrial societies, it is unlikely that such targeting will occur in the foreseeable future.

Given this historical and current situation it is hardly surprising that one commentator can write of disabled people and other groups:

> Their condition or situation makes them economically unproductive and hence economically and socially dependent.
>
> (Illsley, 1981, 328)

This is only partly true, however, for despite the high rates of unemployment in the industrialised world, the majority of those of working age do have a job, and hence are economically productive. In addition, day centres, adult training centres and sheltered workshops make a considerable economic contribution by carrying out jobs that cannot easily be mechanised, at wage rates that make third world workers look expensive. But more importantly, this takes a narrow view of the economy and fails to recognise the importance of consumption. At present the benefits paid to disabled people amounts to some three billion pounds a year (Disability Alliance, 1987) most of which 'will almost invariably be spent to the full' (George and Wilding, 1984). The numbers of firms now producing aids and equipment for disabled people and the seriousness with which motor manufacturers now take disabled motorists are testament to the important and productive role that disabled people play in the economy.

Following Illsley's narrow definition, the British Royal Family can be characterised as economically unproductive and economically and socially dependent. However, it is recognised that the institution of the Monarchy performs an important economic role, and they are not labelled 'dependents', except by their fiercest critics. That disabled people can be so labelled, therefore, is due to a variety of other factors and is not solely a function of inaccurate assumptions about their role in the economy. Some of these other factors will now be considered.

A Political Basis for the Creation of Dependency

Policies enacted through the legislative process also have the effect of creating dependency, and the current restructuring of the British welfare state is legitimated by the desire to reduce our 'culture of dependency'. In the case of disability, both the National Assistance Act (1948) and the Chronically Sick and Disabled Persons Act (1970) aimed to provide services for disabled people and in so doing reinforced

> . . . the notion that people who happen to have disabilities are people who are 'helpless', unable to choose for themselves the aids to opportunity they need.
>
> (Sherear, 1981, 82)

More recently, the Disabled Persons (Services, Consultation and Representation) Act (1986), born out of both a recognition of the inadequacies of previous legislation as well as a wish to involve disabled people more in shaping their own destinies, is underpinned by the desire to improve the services for this dependent group. It offers disabled people the right to be assessed, consulted and represented. However, it is noticeably silent on how these rights can be achieved in the face of recalcitrant local authorities, just as previous legislation was silent on how services could be obtained. In fact, this Act is yet a further extension of the professional and administrative approaches to the problems of disability, rather than an acknowledgement of disability as a human rights issue.

Yet in the aftermath of the Second World War, the Disabled Persons (Employment) Act (1944) recognised that disabled people had a right to work. This legislation was not uninfluenced by the shortage of labour at the time or the collective guilt of seeing ex-service men who had been disabled while fighting for their country; but economic and social climates change, and these rights have never been enforced. Unsuccessful attempts to acknowledge the human rights issue involved have, through the passage of anti-discrimination legislation, surfaced in recent years, but Parliament in its wisdom has never allowed the issue to receive legislative acknowledgement (Oliver, 1985). Thus the legislative framework remains locked into a professional and administrative approach to service provision. The ways in which service provision further perpetuates dependency will be considered in the next section, but before so doing, one further political basis for the creation of dependency needs to be considered.

A further way in which dependency is, at least, reinforced is through the manner in which the discourse with regard to disability and social policy is conducted. From the patronising way politicians discuss disability in Parliament, through the failure of social policy analysts to examine critically the concept of disability (Oliver, 1986), to the failure of policy makers to consult with disabled people, this dependency is reinforced. Nor, indeed, when attention is turned to community care does the discourse alter, for community care implies 'looking after people' (Audit Commission, 1986). The nature of this discourse has recently been criticised thus:

> . . . the need to be 'looked after' may well adequately describe the way potentially physically disabled candidates for 'community care' are perceived by people who are not disabled. This viewpoint has a long history, and a correspondingly successful application in practice – which has led to large numbers of us becoming passive recipients of a wide range of professional and other interventions. But, however good passivity and the creation of dependency may be for the careers of service providers, it is bad news for disabled people and the public purse.
>
> (BCODP, 1987, 3.2)

A Professional Basis for the Creation of Dependency

There are a number of ways in which dependency is created through the delivery of professionalised services. The kinds of services that are available – notably residential and day care facilities with their institutionalised regimes, their failure to involve disabled people meaningfully in the running of such facilities, the transportation of users in specialised transport and the rigidity of the routine activities which take place therein – all serve to institutionalise disabled people and create dependency. While in recent years some attempts have been made to address this problem of dependency creation in these facilities, it is still unfortunately true that power and control continue to remain with professional staff. Many community services are delivered in similar ways and reinforce dependency: disabled people are offered little choice about aids and equipment, times at which professionals can attend to help with matters like toileting, dressing or preparing a meal are restricted, and the limited range of tasks that professionals can perform are further limited because of professional boundaries, employer requirements or trade union practices.

The professional-client relationship can itself also be dependency creating, and indeed the very language used suggests that power is unequally distributed within this relationship. Recent attempts to address this problem through changing the terminology from 'client' to 'user' or 'consumer' acknowledge that the problem exists but do little to change the structures within which these power relations are located. Economic structures determine the roles of professionals as gate-keepers of scarce resources, legal structures determine their controlling functions as administrators of services, career structures determine their decisions about whose side they are actually on and cognitive structures determine their practice with individual disabled people who need help – otherwise, why would they be employed to help them? This is not just another attack on overburdened professionals for they are as much trapped in dependency creation relationships as are their clients. However, all is not as it seems, for in a fundamental sense it is professionals who are dependent upon disabled people. They are dependent on them for their jobs, their salaries, their subsidised transport, their quality of life, and so on.

Thus if disabled people and professionals are trapped in these dependency-creating relationships, is there a way out of the trap? A false start has already been made through the promotion of the goal of independence which figures largely in the interventions of most professionals and the articulated aims of most disabled people. It has been a false start, however, because in advancing the idea of independence, professionals and disabled people have not been talking about the same thing. Professionals tend to define independence in terms of self-care activities such as washing, dressing, toileting, cooking and eating without assistance. Disabled people, however define independence differently, seeing it as the ability to be in control of and make decisions about one's life, rather than doing things alone or without help. Hence it is 'a mind process not contingent upon a normal body' (Huemann, 1983).

If disabled people and professionals are ever going to engage in dependency reducing rather than dependency creating relationships, then the following advice from a disabled sociologist must be taken into account:

> We must expand the notion of independence from physical achievements to sociopsychologic decision-making. Independent living must include not only the quality of physical tasks we can do but the quality of life we can lead. Our notion of human integrity must take into account the notion of taking risks. Rehabilitation personnel must change the model of service from doing something to someone to planning and creating services with someone. In short, we must free ourselves from some of the culture-bound and time-limited standards and philosophy that currently exist.
> (Zola, 1982, 396)

There are, of course, many other ways in which dependency is created, whether these are patronising social attitudes or the inaccessibility of the built environment, which constantly forces disabled people to seek help. There is not the time or space to consider these in detail here, but we need now to consider the disabled individual who stands at the end of these economic, political and professional processes which create dependency.

The Creation of the Dependent Individual

A recent study of a small group of young disabled people attending a further education college found that:

> Many of the students arrive in college with very negative self-image and poor self-esteem. Often they appear to have been conditioned into accepting a devalued social role as sick, pitiful, a burden of charity.
>
> (Hutchinson and Tennyson, 1986, 33)

Precisely how and why these disabled young people came to see themselves in this way now needs to be addressed.

All of the young people studied came to the college from special schools and there is no doubt that the medical hegemony in special education has hardly been challenged by recent legislative changes (Warnock, 1978; Education Act, 1981). In practice, medical need still predominates over educational need; disabled children still have operations (necessary and unnecessary) at times which fit in with the schedules of surgeons and hospitals rather than educational programmes, children are still taken out from classes for doctors appointments or physiotherapy and the school nurse is still a more influential figure than are the teachers. If children are brought up to believe, through experiencing a range of medical and paramedical interventions, that they are ill, we cannot be surprised if they passively accept the sick role.

But it is not only the intrusion of medicine into education which creates dependency through an acceptance of the sick role. They also see themselves as pitiful because they are socialised into accepting disability as a tragedy personal to them. This occurs because teachers, like other professionals, also hold to this view of disability, curriculum materials portray disabled people (if they appear at all) as pathetic victims or arch villains, and their education takes place in a context in which any understanding of the history and politics of disability is absent. The situation has been summarised as follows:

The special education system, then, is one of the main channels for disseminating the predominant able-bodied/minded perception of the world and ensuring that disabled school leavers are socially immature and isolated. This isolation results in passive acceptance of social discrimination, lack of skills in facing the tasks of adulthood and ignorance about the main social issues of our time. All this reinforces the 'eternal children' myth and ensures at the same time disabled school leavers lack the skills for overcoming the myth.

(John, 1986, 6)

However, it is not just the educational environment which creates this dependency: the social environment also plays a significant role in shaping the view that some disabled people hold of themselves as burdens of charity. To begin with, many of the traditional voluntary organisations for disabled people are quite shameless in the way they reinforce this charitable image through their fund-raising campaigns. The prime objective is to maximise income, regardless of the image presented. The unfortunate thing about this is that many of these organisations are not even aware of the way in which this approach creates dependency, and even if they are, then an instrumental, 'ends justifies means' philosophy is used.

But it is not only voluntary organisations who beg on behalf of disabled people; some professionals are even employed by government agencies so to do. For example, disablement resettlement officers (DROs) employed by the Manpower Services Commission, instead of ensuring that employers are carrying out their legal duties under the Disabled Person's (Employment) Act, are given the task of persuading employers to give jobs to disabled people. Perhaps it is a mark of our civilisation in the industrialised world that we employ some people to beg on behalf of others; in many so-called less civilised societies, disabled people are at least accorded the dignity of begging on their own behalf.

Finally, many disabled people are forced into the position of passive recipients of unwanted gifts or inappropriate services, for to refuse such 'generosity' would be to confirm the 'fact' that disabled people have not come to terms with their disability and have a 'chip on their shoulder'. Examples of unwanted or unsuitable gifts are the wheelchairs designed by Lord Snowdon which turned out to be unusable by anyone who is paralysed; and examples of inappropriate services are the special vehicles, usually with the name of the donor written large all over the side, which are often used to transport disabled people. These are particularly used to carry disabled people to and from segregated facilities such as special schools, day centres and residential homes.

So far, I have shown how dependency is created amongst disabled people, not because of the effects of the functional limitations on their capacities for self-care, but because their lives are shaped by a variety of economic, political and social forces which produces this dependency. And dependency is not a problem simply for the dependent individual, but also for politicians, planners and professionals who have to manage (control) this dependency in accordance with current social values and economic circumstances. It is these issues which now need to be considered.

The Restructuring of the Welfare State – The Elimination of Dependency

Since the mid 1970s there has been a world economic recession, one result of which has been to call into question both the nature and future of welfare states in the industrial world. This questioning has usually been raised within the language of crisis, of which there are at least three dimensions:

(a) a crisis in the welfare state in that it was not meeting social needs;
(b) a crisis of the welfare state in that it was creating needs that it could not meet;
(c) a crisis by the welfare state in that the rising cost of welfare was creating a crisis of capitalism itself.

Further,

The crisis definition is now being used as an ideological basis for reducing social expenditure, changing redistributive patterns in disfavour of the marginal groups and reducing government responsibility in social policy.

(Oyen, 1986, 6)

While both the precise nature of this crisis and the ideological response to it differs from industrial country to industrial country, all have had broadly similar experiences. In Britain, the left have broadly subscribed to the view that there is a crisis in the welfare state and that the solution is to increase public expenditure on it. The right, on the other hand, have subscribed to the view that there is a crisis of the welfare state and, if not properly managed and controlled, it could indeed become a crisis of the capitalist state. As the right have held political power for most of this period, it is their view of the nature of the crisis which has shaped the process of restructuring the welfare state. A major underpinning of the ideological basis for this restructuring has been the issue of dependency. Reductions in expenditure, changes in redistribution and the gradual withdrawal of the state from people's lives, have all been legitimated on the grounds of the need to reduce dependency.

There is little doubt, with regard to disabled people, that their experiences of the welfare state coincide with both the 'crisis in' and 'crisis of' dimensions. In other words, they have not received all the services they need and in many cases those services that they have received have created or reinforced their dependency. So, it has to be said that future policy options stemming from either (or both) of these dimensions are unlikely to succeed in reducing dependency, whether it be physical or social. Simply increasing public expenditure will only serve to lock disabled people further into the dependency creating relationships I have already described, and reductions and redistributions will condemn disabled people to isolation and loneliness in the community or institutionalisation in residential care. This raises the issue of what, if anything, can be done to ease this crisis as far as disabled people are concerned.

In the preceding analysis I have given primacy to the economic basis for creating dependency, but it has to be concluded that in the current political climate, there is little scope for intervening in the economy, for

> Social policy has been assigned . . . to the role of intervening in a natural order of economic relationships to modify their outcome in the interests of 'social' goals. In both capitalist and state socialist societies, social policy has operated as a 'handmaiden' to the economy.
>
> (Walker, 1984, 33)

Hence the chances of tackling this economic basis for the creation of dependency amongst disabled people 'are slim because the same societal forces which manufacture disability also mitigate against a structural response' (Borsay, 1986, 188).

Even allowing for this pessimistic scenario, there are a number of things which can be done to tackle the political and professional bases for dependency creation amongst disabled people, and it is these which will now be considered. So far, the political right have been making the running and their main strategy has been to resolve the 'crisis of' the welfare state by tackling the problems of dependency creation through the privatisation of state services. There are also a number of strategies that could be adopted by the left to tackle the 'crisis in' the welfare state and these will be discussed. These strategies are the introduction of anti-discrimination legislation, freedom of information and the proper financial and other support of organisations controlled and run by disabled people themselves.

Currently, therefore, the strategy of privatisation, underpinned by the rhetoric of targeting, consumer choice and dependency reduction is the dominant one. As far as disabled people are concerned, this privatisation is not something that has occurred only in recent years. Services such as residential care and special education have been provided by organisations like the Cheshire Foundation and the Spastics Society almost since the inception of the welfare state, and all the evidence suggests that these services create dependency in exactly the same way as state services. More recently the privatisation of some cash payments for some severely disabled people (who would previously have had statutory rights to such payments through the establishment of a trust fund to be administered by the Disablement Income Group) is only likely to reinforce dependency by furthering the image of disabled people as burdens of charity.

It is, perhaps, ironic that the model for providing these privatised services is that of the supermarket; the argument being that packages of care can be purchased just as customers purchase products from supermarket shelves. Ironic because many disabled people find shopping in supermarkets difficult if not impossible because of physical access, difficulties in reaching shelves and the fact that products and packaging are tailored to the needs of the modern nuclear family and not to the needs of individuals. In short, supermarkets offer a limited range of products which suit the needs of particular groups in society and if not in these groups, then the consumer is not 'king', as the rhetoric would have it. Thus, for many disabled people, the supermarket model of provision is unlikely to offer anything substantially different from the provision of state services; that is to say, little choice over what is provided and little control over how it is provided.

What the supermarket is alleged to offer, but clearly does not, is choice and control. The key issue for the future as far as the left is concerned is whether the 'crisis in' the welfare state can be resolved by offering users of services choice and control. I want to suggest that, by the modification and adaptation of first principles, it can:

> The challenge that faces us is not the choice between universalist and selective services. The real challenge resides in the question: what particular infrastructure of universalist services is needed in order to provide a framework of values and opportunity bases within and around which can be developed acceptable selective services provided as social rights, on criteria of needs of specific

categories, groups and territorial areas and not dependent upon individual tests of means?

(Titmuss, 1968, 122)

To update the language somewhat, it should be possible to allow for choice and control in service provision within a universalist infrastructure, if consumers have social rights to these services and if there are mechanisms whereby the needs of groups and communities, whether local or interest communities, can be articulated by them themselves.

It has become clear that if disabled people are to have social rights to services, then the legislative framework must do more than simply list these services (Chronically Sick and Disabled Person's Act) or provide professional and administrative approaches to their provision (Disabled Person's [Services, Consultation and Representation] Act). This inevitably implies the necessity for anti-discrimination legislation which would not only provide public affirmation of the unacceptability of discrimination against disabled people, but also, if properly drafted, a framework for the enforcement of service delivery and a mechanism for professional accountability.

By itself it would not be enough, of course, as the experience in the areas of race and gender demonstrate. Therefore an essential adjunct would be legislation facilitating complete freedom of information which goes beyond current attempts to provide access to information held on computers and in local authority files. The locked medical cabinets would need to be opened and the unofficial documents that are kept as ways of avoiding information disclosure would (as with current practices which require information to be provided to parents under the statementing regulations of the Education Act [1981]) need to be made available.

Finally, a mechanism whereby the needs of groups and communities can be articulated needs to be developed. This can only be accomplished through the adequate funding and resourcing of organisations controlled and run by disabled people, which have been going from strength to strength throughout the world in the 1980s. Significantly, there is some evidence that these organisations of disabled people find it easier to flourish in the under-developed rather than the industrial world. This is due, in part, to the resistance to change of bureaucratic and professional structures in the industrial world but also to the existence of a large and powerful sector of traditional organisations for the disabled who remain locked into dependency creating service provision and attitudes, and who, consequently, have vested interests in maintaining the status quo.

None of these developments by themselves, or an incremental approach to them, are likely to prove successful. Anti-discrimination legislation without freedom of information and a supportive network of disabled people will simply mean that the lawyers will get rich; freedom of information by itself will mean that individual disabled people will be subjected to professional mystification and sleight of hand; and support for the disabled people's movement without a framework which guarantees basic human rights will leave the movement politically emasculated. But an integrated programme, as suggested above, could provide a means of addressing the problems of dependency creation at both political and professional levels, and hence go some way to resolving the 'crises' both in, and of, the welfare state, at least as far as disabled people are concerned.

Conclusions

An inevitable consequence of living in industrial society is that we all live in a condition of mutual dependency. However the dichotomy of dependence/independence has been a significant influence on both the way disabled people are perceived in general and on the development of social policies geared towards them in particular. Dependency is created by a variety of economic, political, professional and other forces, and recent changes in the structure of the welfare state have been legitimated on the grounds of the need to reduce this dependency. Policies based upon the 'crisis in' the welfare state thesis are unlikely to succeed in reducing dependency, though they may temporarily resolve the crisis of capitalism created by public expenditure on the welfare state.

Ultimately, only attempts to tackle the 'crisis of' the welfare state are likely to be successful, for the creation of an infrastructure of state services which facilitate user choice and control is the only way in which dependency can be permanently removed. While this will be more costly for the capitalist economy in the short term, it may not only prevent such a crisis of capitalism from occurring, but will also create a much happier environment for us all to live in a state of mutual interdependence.

References

Albrecht, G. and Levy J. (1981) 'Constructing Disabilities as Social Problems in Albrecht, G. (Ed) *Cross National Rehabilitation Policies: A Sociological Perspective*, London, Sage.

Audit Commission (1986) *Making a Reality of Community Care*, London, HMSO.

Borsay, A. (1986) 'Personal Trouble or Public Issue? Towards a model of policy for people with physical and mental disabilities' *Disability, Handicap and Society*, 1, 2.

BCODP – British Council of Organisations of Disabled People (1987) *Comment on the Report of the Audit Commission*, London, BCODP.

Disability Alliance (1987) *Poverty and Disability: Breaking the link*, London, London Disability Alliance.

Erlanger, H. and Roth, W. (1985) 'Disability Policy: The Parts and the Whole', *American Behavioural Scientist*, 28, 3.

George, V. and Wilding, P. (1984) *The Impact of Social Policy*, London, Routledge and Kegan Paul.

Hahn, H. (1985) 'Disability Policy and the Problem of Discrimination', *American Behavioural Scientist*, 28, 3.

Hahn, H. (1986) 'Public Support for Rehabilitation Programs: the Analysis of US Disability Policy' *Disability, Handicap and Society*, 1, 2.

Heumann, J. (1983) Quoted in Crewe, N. and Zola, I. *Independent Living for Physically Disabled People*, London, Jossey-Bass.

Hutchinson, D. and Tennyson, C. (1986) *Transition to Adulthood*, London, Further Education Unit.

Illsley, R. (1981) 'Problems of Dependency groups: the care of the elderly, the handicapped and the chronically ill, *Social Science and Medicine* 15a, 3 (Part II).

John, M. (1986) *Disabled Young People Living Independently*, London, British Council of Organisations of Disabled People.

Manning, N. (Ed.) (1985) *Social Problems and Welfare Ideology*, Aldershot, Gower.

Oliver, M. (1985) 'Discrimination, Disability and Social Policy' in Brenton, M. and Jones, C. *The Year Book of Social Policy in Britain 1984–5*, London, Routledge and Kegan Paul.

Oliver, M. (1986) 'Disability and Social Policy: Some Theoretical Issues', *Disability, Handicap and Society*, 1, 1.

Oyen, E. (Ed) (1986) *Comparing Welfare States and Their Futures*, Aldershot, Gower.

Ryan, J. and Thomas F.(1980) *The Politics of Mental Handicap*, Harmondsworth, Penguin.

Titmuss, R. (1968) *Commitment to Welfare*, London, Allen and Unwin.

Walker, A. (1984) 'The Political Economy of Privatisation' in Le Grand, J. and Robinson, R. (Ed) *Privatisation and the Welfare State*, London, Allen and Unwin.

Wilding, P. (1982) *Professional Power and Social Welfare*, London, Routledge and Kegan Paul.

Zola, I. (1982) 'Social and Cultural Disincentives to Independent Living' *Archives of Physical Medicine and Rehabilitation*, 63.

Chapter Two

Human Service Policies: The Rhetoric Versus The Reality

Wolf Wolfensberger

The field of organisational dynamics deals with both how people behave within organisations, and how entire organisations themselves behave. However, its insights also apply to other social systems, including closely interlinked sets of organisations, such as government, which *de facto* function much as if they were a single organisation.

The insights of organisational dynamics are as relevant to the human service field as they are elsewhere. They apply not only to discrete service agencies or voluntary associations that are concerned with some aspect of human service, but also to the entire service sector, and to various service fields and professional organisations within it. In many societies, human services are *de facto* shaped and steered by an overall pattern of policies, structures and practices which are remarkably consistent with each other across local communities, agencies, fields, and professions. This pattern is what I call the 'human service supersystem'. It can also be viewed as being a paradigm – at least, a superparadigm. The service system as a whole is thus much like an organisation. The reason this human service supersystem is relatively consistent throughout all of what one might call its 'regions' is relatively obvious: the service supersystem overwhelmingly reflects the larger culture within which it functions, and its control mechanisms. In fact, there has been such a convergence of cultural patterns taking place in recent decades that even the human services of separate nations reflect the same controlling influences.

One thing that all groups and organisations have in common is a tendency to function unconsciously, i.e., they may perform functions, or pursue goals, or have processes, of which the members, and commonly also observers, are unaware. Not only that, but even worse, a language may develop that actually proclaims the opposite of what is going on, which usually deepens the prevailing unconsciousness of the organisational realities. The organisational literature uses two terms to encapture this reality, at least as it pertains to the functions of organisations. Namely, it speaks of 'manifest' and 'latent' organisational functions.

Manifest functions are the obvious, apparent, and usually stated ones. In human services, these appear to have something to do with meeting the needs of the people served, and to allay all sorts of afflictions and miseries. These goals are also almost universally those that human service organisations, and their functionaries, publicly proclaim. Schools claim to be educational, residential institutions to be habilitative or at least kindly sheltering, psychotherapists to be alleviating mental anguish or mental disorder, etc.

In contrast, latent functions are those which are hidden, unannounced, underlying, and implicit rather than stated. Often, members of an organisation or field are not even conscious that their organisation or field has and plays these functions, though they are nonetheless utterly real, and possibly even of overarching proportions.

It is awesome to contemplate that, commonly, it is not the manifest functions that are proclaimed by almost everyone that are the real, or at least major, functions of a social body, but the latent ones, and that the proclaimed manifest functions may be entirely untrue, or contain only an element of truth. Indeed, it is the latent functions that so often carry out an unproclaimed, unconscious mission on behalf of the larger society, or of a specific segment thereof.

A major problem with social systems generally is that the people within them are largely unconscious of many of the major realities concerning the social system of which they are part, including its latent functions. Further, the more complex the social system, the less consciousness there usually prevails within and about it, and the more do its members voice inaccurate beliefs about the nature, function, functioning, mission, purpose, outcome, etc., of that system. If the real functions and outputs of a social system are contrary to the positive ideals of most of its members, then unconsciousness is virtually guaranteed to be high, and deception even more widely prevalent. For instance, if one's highest belief system calls one to be peaceful, to love, to build, etc., but a system with which one is intimately identified is violent or destructive, then persons who remain part of such a system over any length of time are overwhelmingly likely to reinterpret the bad things that their system is and does as reflecting their nobler values and intents, and they are overwhelmingly likely to deny – indeed, to run away from – the unpleasant gruesome truth.

The psychologist Seymour Sarason has written widely (e.g. 1969, 1972) about what he calls 'the creation of settings.' In this context, 'setting' refers to much more than just a physical facility, but also to its broader social context or atmosphere. He says that the ideologies and purposes that prevail when a setting is first created – whether these are conscious or unconscious – will shape what that setting is like not only at its beginning but pretty much for the rest of its existence. This can work for either good or bad.

One way to think of this is to say that settings, including organisations, have ghosts spooking within them. These ghosts may be good or evil spirits, and are the ways of thinking and doing things of the founder figures and era.

Another relevant maxim is very similar to Sarason's idea. It is that organisations can only be understood if one understands the 'contingencies' that prevailed when they were founded. For instance, if a service pattern was founded during a time when the people to be served were viewed as a serious threat to society, then all sorts of elements of that service pattern will reflect this perception. The service building might have been constructed with high walls around it, many heavy locked doors, and bars on the windows. Staff may have been called guards, and carried weapons and many keys. The clients may have been dressed in prison-type uniforms, and had to follow prison-type routines. As a result, many years later – even centuries later – the 'spoor' of this early ideology and these earlier practices may linger on, even if the people are not a menace at all or are no longer perceived as such. Indeed, they may linger on when the building is used by an entirely different client group and staffed by people who have no idea of what the founding precepts were. For instance, a male staff supervisor might still be called 'captain.'

Similarly, if an organisation was founded during a time when deep suspicion of government prevailed, then various elements of that organisation will continue to reflect this suspicion. For instance, the founding documents of the organisation may have spelled out certain strategies of distantiating the organisation from government (e.g., in funding). Public officials may be prohibited from holding any office, or even from being members of the organisation. New employees and members may be indoctrinated with a profound skepticism of anything promoted by or coming from government, and so on. Even if it should come to pass that these apprehensions are no longer relevant, their traditions will almost certainly linger, and be passed down from generation to new generation of workers and members. Thus, any organisation is deeply influenced, and even controlled, by past contingencies of which its present members may have zero awareness or understanding.

Because latent functions constitute an unconscious driving force, they are a major source of distortions, perversions and troubles. Thus, a major goal of organisational adaptation should be to identify latent goals as they start sprouting, and either convert them into legitimate manifest ones, or get rid of them. A second major goal of organisational adaptation should be to try to gain conscious control over these unconscious goals, so that they do not end up controlling the organisation, which would be a clear instance of the cart leading the horse.

However, while latent functions might be divided into those which are virtually never acknowledged as legitimate, and those which might be acknowledged as legitimate by some organisations, but which are not acknowledged as such by the one at issue, very few organisations ever really come to grips with their latent functions, in good part because the cost (in the broadest sense of the term) of doing so is so great. It may require confronting a very painful reality, discomfiting powerful members or patrons, making a conscious decision as to whether to continue to pursue a less-than-noble goal, etc. All these things are apt to introduce strife, even division, and separation of some members from the group, which all groups tend to resist.

One of the best ways to identify what the latent functions, as well as the weaknesses – and even potential sources of downfall – of a social system are, is to discover what realities are strenuously excluded from explicated address and conversation by and within that system. In closely-knit communities (and thus communalities), identification of undercurrents of discontent, or even personality conflicts, are commonly taboo, and yet it is precisely these things which eventually break up such communities. In enlightened liberal circles, for example, it is virtually impossible to discuss feminism in any terms other than those of the prevailing 'normal' feminism, and its negative features and impacts are taboo.

When a social system (including an entire society) is strong and secure, it may be able to tolerate a discussion of weaknesses and potential trouble spots, but one that sees itself at risk, or that is even in a state of collapse, will be particularly likely to exclude any such discussion, and in a sense prefers its own death to any discussion of the fact that this death is about to occur.

In the human service field, we are confronted by a great deal of rhetoric, and by an avalanche of documents, that proclaim that services are beneficent, charitable, benign, curative, habilitative, etc. These then are the manifest functions of human service organisations. But while services may be some of these things some of the time, they also commonly perform latent functions very different from these proclaimed ones, including ones that are competency-impairing, destructive of independence, that are actually dependency-making and dependency-keeping, health-debilitating, and outright death-accelerating, and thus killing. Unfortunately, people in human services have done extremely poorly in learning to distinguish between such manifest and latent functions, even when they have learned to be otherwise very sophisticated about organisational dynamics. This presentation will look at this issue in further detail.

By their very nature, many types of organisations are constrained in regard to the kinds of claims that they may credibly make. For instance, a cigarette factory may claim that it makes cigarettes that add some pleasure to people's lives, and it might described these pleasures in terms such as generation of a pleasant aroma, giving people a 'high', stimulating their concentration, giving them more sex appeal, etc. But by and large, such claims are rather modest, and are universally recognised as leaning toward 'hype'. Should the factory claim to be making baby bottles while really making cigarettes, it would be ridiculed, discredited, and almost certainly put out of business. A firm that makes ball bearings will only be able to say a few good things about what it does.

In contrast, human services have traditionally been interpreted as moral enterprises of great positive impact on those on whom they are bestowed. Thus, there is hardly a noble claim from human services that has *not* been made at one time or another, all the way up to the claim in recent years – perhaps not so noble – that human services (such as medicine) will soon conquer ageing and all diseases, and make human beings immortal. Yet from a study of history and a close observation of contemporary services, those whose minds have not been encaptured by the mainstream epistemology find it quite easy to identify all sorts of hidden functions served by human service organisations and fields that are anything *but* noble.

For example, one can point to any number of instances where a human service was initiated, or at least funded, primarily in order to serve the latent function of bringing glory and recognition to a funder or donor, rather than to serve the manifest function of benefiting its clients. Similarly, whenever a human service building or agency is named after an important personage, honoring this personage has thereby become at least one of the functions of the service, though in most cases it is not likely that this will be overtly acknowledged. However, this example is not too alarming because it might still be possible for a service to carry out the major part of its manifest functions even while serving its latent one.

One striking recent example of the discrepancy between social policy rhetoric and social policy decision-making was uncovered by Farel (1988). She obtained the state developmental disabilities plans of the period 1984–86 from apparently all the US states, and then identified 27 of the states' plans as having designated child development as a priority service area. She then analysed the percentage of the money that was available to developmental disabilities councils that was actually allocated by them to child development projects, and correlated these with various indices of child distress or unmet needs. The correlations all hovered round 0, and the author concluded that there was no relationship between declared priorities and actual allocations, despite the fact that developmental disabilities councils are now made up of about 50 per cent of handicapped people or their family members.

However, an example of human service where the manifest and latent functions were totally opposed to one another to the great injury of the clients was a so-called nursing home prevention service for elderly people. The manifest function was to help elderly people remain independent and healthy so that they would not become debilitated and have to enter a nursing home. However, that its latent real function was exactly the opposite was revealed by the following:

(a) The program was located in a nursing home.

(b) The lay-out of the facility was exceedingly confusing, and would therefore cause its clients to become confused, and/or to believe that they were confused.

(c) Almost every clock on the walls showed a different time, and similarly, every publicly visible calendar displayed a different date, all of which could not help but disorient the clients already at risk.

(d) The doors were so built that only very strong persons could open them, which would make clients think that they were becoming weak and feeble.

(e) The decorations, activities, and schedule were all childish and trivial, thereby casting the elderly clients into roles of diminished activity, 'second childhood,' and so on.

As a result of all these things, clients of the program were actually highly apt to end up disoriented, confused, less healthy, and less independent, than if they had not been clients in this service at all! Sophisticated observers could thus recognise this service as having a feeder function for the local nursing homes, in both impairing elderly people so that everyone could agree that they 'needed' a nursing home, and in making the identification and induction of people into available nursing home places convenient for human service personnel.

We gain further insight here if we contemplate that in each society, there are certain groups of people who, as groups, are largely disliked, devalued and rejected by the majority of the society. Most of these devalued groups have been devalued for centuries. In our society, as in most Western ones, these devalued groups are the following: the mentally retarded; the mentally disordered; people with physical handicaps; people with epilepsy; people with sensory handicaps; severely and/or chronically ill people; people who have offended against the law, or who are in prison, or hold politically unpopular views; people who are poor; minority groups and people who may not be fully assimilated into the culture because of their racial, ethnic, or religious backgrounds; and people who are elderly.

It is largely the devalued groups I have just enumerated who have been defined by society as 'needing' human services. In fact, they may be said to 'need' peculiar 'services' such as the following:

(a) They may be said to 'need' to be institutionalised.

(b) They may be said to 'need' bizarre and injurious treatments.

(c) It may be said that it is in their best interest if they died, and that they thus have a 'need' to be killed.

(d) Conversely, people may be interpreted as themselves needing to kill, or at least as needing to have it done on their behalf by a human service, as when a pregnant woman is said to 'need' an abortion.

It is because the major functions of social systems, and organisations especially, are so typically not only not announced, but not even recognised, known or acknowledged by them and their functionaries, that social scientists have warned that one cannot identify the true purposes, goals and functions of an organisation from an examination of organisational rhetoric, i.e., from what the organisation says about itself, either via its leaders and spokespersons, or its documents (constitutions, by-laws, descriptive flyers, pubic relations releases, etc.). Instead, the only reliable means of learning what an organisation is really up to, and what its true goals, purposes and functions are, is by observing it over a prolonged period of time, and noting what it is actually doing, i.e., what its actual characteristic behavior and output is.

This brings us to the crucial question: what are the major latent but real functions played by the human service system in our society today? In order to answer this question, we must do three things:

(a) We must look at human services in their entirety, or at least at the entirety of major sectors thereof. We must not be distracted by looking only at specific agencies or locales.

(b) We must look at what an entirety of services actually accomplishes.

(c) We must not be influenced or distracted by what is said or written by politicians, service organisations, professional organisations, or individual human service workers or leaders, or even in the law.

If we do this, and are not sidetracked by rhetoric, we find an answer that is shocking and unpleasant. Because it is so unpleasant, it is extremely controverted, though it is amazingly easy to demonstrate. The answer is that the major function of contemporary human services is to support a post-agricultural and post-industrial, and therefore 'post-primary production', economy. We will now explain what this means.

Largely since the end of World War II, and largely as a result of technological developments, there has been a transformation in the economic structure of Western societies; namely, the economy has changed from one in which the vast majority of the population was engaged in primary production – i.e. farming, fishing, mining, manufacturing, and construction, the things which produce what we need in order to live – into one in which only a very small proportion of the populace is engaged in such labor, and even that small proportion is decreasing. Thus, we have entered a post-primary production economic era, which we abbreviate as PPP, in which human services play a crucial but very hidden/latent function. Figures 1 and 2 illustrate this.

Until relatively recently, the production of basic goods, mostly needed for relatively short-term survival, absorbed the vast majority of human labor, and supported a small tip of leisure, culture, art, and other nonproductive pursuits. Today, the more developed a society is, the more this ancient pattern is turned upside down.

In the United States at least, the PPP phenomenon resulted in a mere 20 per cent of the labor force in 1983 engaged in some form of primary production, and the agricultural sector (as of circa 1984) was down to only 5 per cent of the labor force, and thus constituted only 25 per cent of the productive labor force. And even in this sector, only about half were actually farmers. Further declines have taken place since then, and the total primary production labor force in the US is predicted to be down to 10 per cent by the year 2000. Similar figures, or at least trends, obtain for other nations in the developed world.

If only 10–20 per cent of the people produce all the wealth – the food we eat, the clothes we wear, the shelter over us, the goods that we can otherwise enjoy – this presents, among others, the following two problems:

(a) If the primary producers of the wealth were permitted to keep the proceeds of all the wealth they produce, then they, and probably only they, would be rich, and everyone else would be poor and dependent, and perhaps 'on welfare'.

Figure 1

THE HISTORIAL PATTERNS OF LABOR

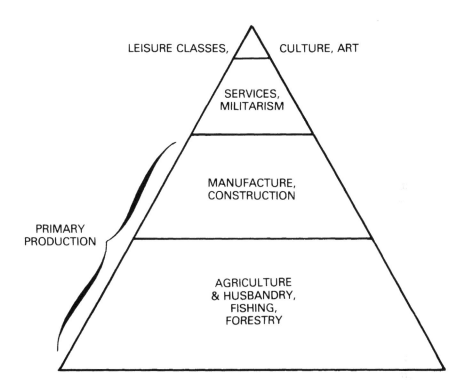

(b) If so few people are engaged in producing goods, then how is one going to occupy the rest of the labor force?

Conceivably, one could allow the primary producers to keep the profits of their labors by setting whatever prices they want for them – but, as we all know, that has not happened. In fact, it is the very primary producers who are being forced by various shenanigans into economic marginality and even outright poverty: for example, witness what is happening to the farmers, the fishers, and to many blue-collar laborers, such as miners.

The strategy that Western society has *de facto* adopted – though largely unconsciously – is to oppress the primary producers, keep them poor or nearly so, take away the fruits of their labor at artificially low prices, create unproductive employment for the rest of the population, and create

Figure 2

OUR POST-PRIMARY PRODUCTION PATTERNS OF LABOR

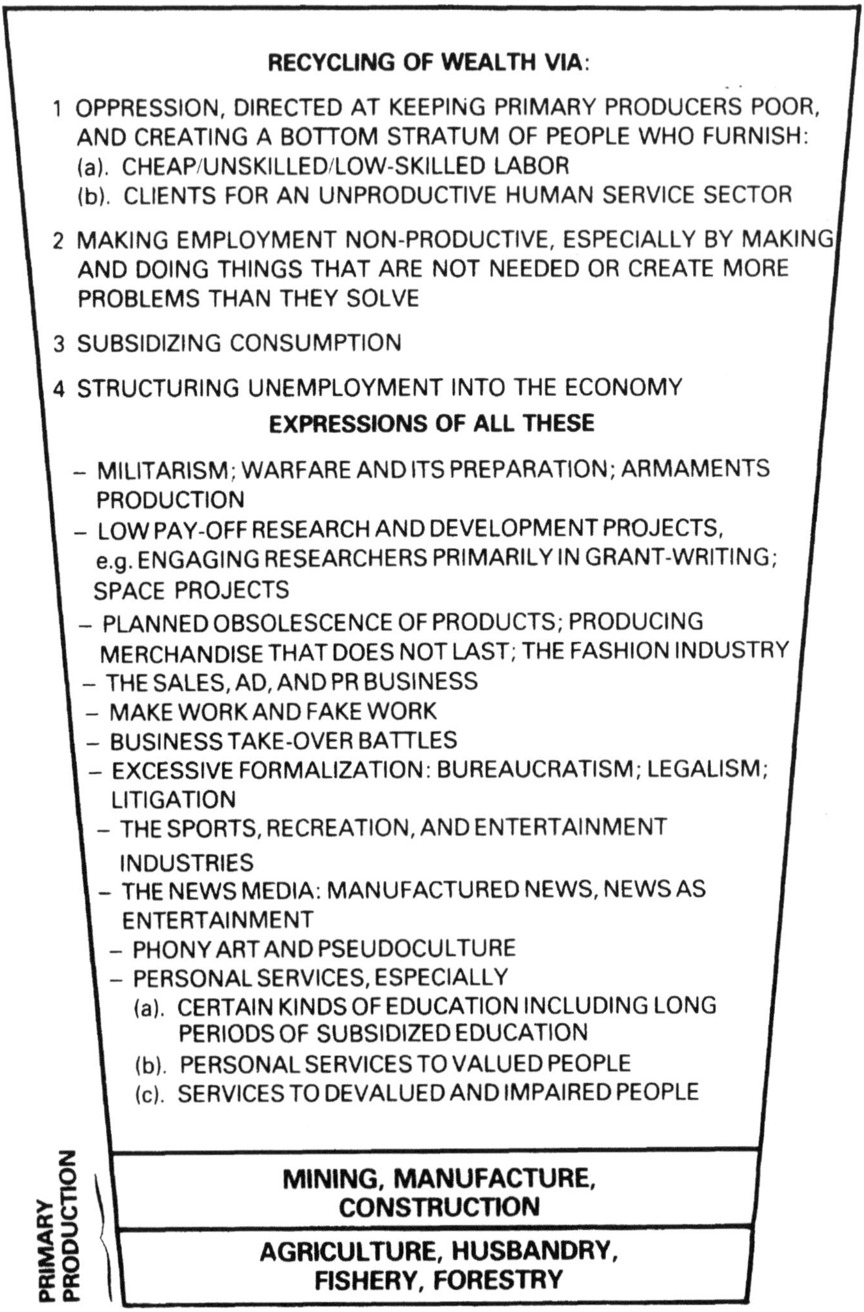

RECYCLING OF WEALTH VIA:

1 OPPRESSION, DIRECTED AT KEEPING PRIMARY PRODUCERS POOR, AND CREATING A BOTTOM STRATUM OF PEOPLE WHO FURNISH:
  (a). CHEAP/UNSKILLED/LOW-SKILLED LABOR
  (b). CLIENTS FOR AN UNPRODUCTIVE HUMAN SERVICE SECTOR

2 MAKING EMPLOYMENT NON-PRODUCTIVE, ESPECIALLY BY MAKING AND DOING THINGS THAT ARE NOT NEEDED OR CREATE MORE PROBLEMS THAN THEY SOLVE

3 SUBSIDIZING CONSUMPTION

4 STRUCTURING UNEMPLOYMENT INTO THE ECONOMY

EXPRESSIONS OF ALL THESE

- MILITARISM; WARFARE AND ITS PREPARATION; ARMAMENTS PRODUCTION
- LOW PAY-OFF RESEARCH AND DEVELOPMENT PROJECTS, e.g. ENGAGING RESEARCHERS PRIMARILY IN GRANT-WRITING; SPACE PROJECTS
- PLANNED OBSOLESCENCE OF PRODUCTS; PRODUCING MERCHANDISE THAT DOES NOT LAST; THE FASHION INDUSTRY
- THE SALES, AD, AND PR BUSINESS
- MAKE WORK AND FAKE WORK
- BUSINESS TAKE-OVER BATTLES
- EXCESSIVE FORMALIZATION: BUREAUCRATISM; LEGALISM; LITIGATION
- THE SPORTS, RECREATION, AND ENTERTAINMENT INDUSTRIES
- THE NEWS MEDIA: MANUFACTURED NEWS, NEWS AS ENTERTAINMENT
- PHONY ART AND PSEUDOCULTURE
- PERSONAL SERVICES, ESPECIALLY
  (a). CERTAIN KINDS OF EDUCATION INCLUDING LONG PERIODS OF SUBSIDIZED EDUCATION
  (b). PERSONAL SERVICES TO VALUED PEOPLE
  (c). SERVICES TO DEVALUED AND IMPAIRED PEOPLE

PRIMARY PRODUCTION

MINING, MANUFACTURE, CONSTRUCTION

AGRICULTURE, HUSBANDRY, FISHERY, FORESTRY

and maintain a large class of the population that is unemployed, and whose reduced identity and oppression provides employment to another whole class of the populace. All of this is done in such subtle and seemingly legitimate-appearing ways that hardly anyone recognises it for what it is. We will now give just a few examples of how this is done, and of how the historical patterns of labor have been up-ended.

In a number of developed countries, the biggest single boost to the economy right now comes from the military sector. Militarism and arms production use up an awful lot of raw material which the primary producers produce; it employs a large number of people in research and development, and in manufacturing and deploying the hardware – and then all of this quickly gets scrapped by the development of newer, more powerful, more expensive and more consumptive weapons; and it keeps the entire soldiery out of the labor market.

Another example is the promotion and institutionalisation of wasteful patterns of consumption. This involves waste on the part of the producers, as in making things that do not last, or that are absolutely worthless, or that are not needed, such as new fashions every year when the old ones are still perfectly good. It also involves the inculcation of wastefulness into consumers, who spend untold billions on items they do not need (e.g., the tenth pair of shoes), that are just plain useless (e.g., 'pet rocks'), or that are outright harmful (such as cigarettes or drugs). So wasteful has our society become that we are literally drowning in all of these things that get thrown out. Predictions are that soon there simply will not be any place left to put all the garbage that we make each day. Also, primary production is so conducted as to pollute the environment, requiring 20 to 200 times the cost to clean it up later than to prevent the pollution in the first place.

Other examples are business take-over battles, and various stock market manipulations. All the people involved in these actions are in the unproductive sector – i.e., they do not fish, farm, mine, manufacture or otherwise produce goods, or even labor – but they profit very handsomely from the primary production of others. And the professions in upper management levels of business, the lawyers, the stockbrokers, are burgeoning while the productive sector is shrinking.

Another example is bureaucratisation. The more formal, organised, and bureaucratised things become, the more people are required in order to manage the complexity, and the more these people strive very hard not to get anything done, and not to let anyone else get anything done. Again, this occupies unimaginable numbers of people, it occupies them in unproductive paid work, and it uses up resources at an unimaginable rate (think only of how much paper is involved!). This particular example is also very apparent in human services, because every day, formal organised human services (such as service agencies, both public and private ones) are subjected to more and more formalisms, requirements and regulations to the point where hardly anybody can do anything for the clients anymore.

These are just a few examples, but of special relevance to us is how human services participate in a PPP economy. By defining ever more human conditions as requiring human service, and especially paid, trained and professional human service, one can create a 'need' for ever more human service workers. Thus, we are witnessing the redefinition of age-old problems of living – growing old, grieving the loss of a loved one, having a hard time coping with the demands of schooling, inability to control one's eating or gambling or sex drive – as being diseases for which one must receive special treatment by professional paid human services. Also, by defining all these people as human service clients, one keeps many of them out of the labor force, and therefore reduces the number of people that one has to occupy unproductively.

But merely enlarging the human service empire is not sufficient to meet all the requirements that a post-primary production economy poses. In addition, one has to make all the services that do exist as unproductive as possible – indeed, one has to make them counterproductive if at all possible, so that they create dependency, and so that they create impaired people, rather than habilitate them. After all, if more people were habilitated, then they would again present a problem of how to occupy not only them, but also the people who used to be kept occupied serving them. Thus it turns out that, in fact, the net product of the contemporary service system is more dependent people, and people who are more dependent, even though there are always a few people somewhere who get habilitated into greater independence and competence, thus serving as a cover or front for the service supersystem.

While most human service workers have no difficulty perceiving some of the other ways we have explained of circulating the wealth and employing people in unproductive work (such as militarism and the inciting of consumerism), they often have difficulty acknowledging the truth of what we have just proposed about organised human services – and for obvious reasons, because to admit this would pose all sorts of moral dilemmas of the most wrenching type to them. Thus, in case there are any skeptics, we will now give a few specific examples of what we have posited.

One current example of what a PPP society does to convert its labor force into human service clients is the following. First, the US asbestos industry injured several hundred thousand of its workers through its unsafe practices, and thereby put them into the unemployed, sick, depen-

dent category that needs vast amounts of human services. Then the lawyers stepped in, and now there are – believe it or not – 25,000 injury
lawsuits pending against thirty-nine asbestos companies, which in turn
are suing sixty-five insurance firms. All this occupies about as many well-
paid lawyers and paper people as injured workers. So far, 63 per cent of
all injury awards have gone to the lawyers, and by the time this is over,
the percentage could rise to about 90 per cent, according to some estimates.

That a 'need' for human services must be manufactured in order to
justify the creation of more and more services and service jobs is dramatically highlighted by an incident in Boston, Massachusetts, where a police-
man and a number of accomplices were found to have lit twenty-nine
fires, including six in a single night. They did this after the passage of a
referendum (Proposition 2½) which limited state spending, and resulted
in layoffs in police and fire departments, and their stated intention was to
'increase public demand for fire-fighters and public safety personnel'.
Much as fire-fighters and police officers are apt to light fires to keep their
jobs, so human services and service workers are apt to light human service
fires, so to speak, in order to keep people dependent so that they will
need human services.

Figure 3 shows that between 1962 and 1986, there was very little increase
in the amount of money that the US government channeled to people
with low incomes. In contrast, the money it allocated to services for them
went up almost five-fold. The message? 'Let them eat services'. Further,
90 per cent of the new jobs created between 1983–1986 in the US have
been in the service sector.

Human service inefficiency is one splendid way of circulating wealth.
One US study found that the sheltered workshops most likely to be
funded were those that had the highest operating costs and the least
evidence of effectiveness. A 1984 article called the British benefit structure
'a ragbag of provisions based on a variety of principles, some of them
relating to a bygone social order . . . that affects disabled people in a
complex, uncoordinated irrational way.' (Croxen and Finkelstein, 1984).

Obviously, if human services were truly productive, then clients would
be habilitated, would no longer need human services, the service system
would collapse, and all the workers who make their living at it would be
out of work, and largely unqualified for any other type of employment.
If a magic solution were found so that there were no more blindness,
deafness, retardation, etc., individual deviancy-managers would go into
poverty because managing deviancy – and managing it nonhabilitationally
– is all that most of them qualify for. For example, if every dollar that
had been given to the US 'war on poverty' in the 1960s and '70s had
instead been given to families below the poverty line, there would not

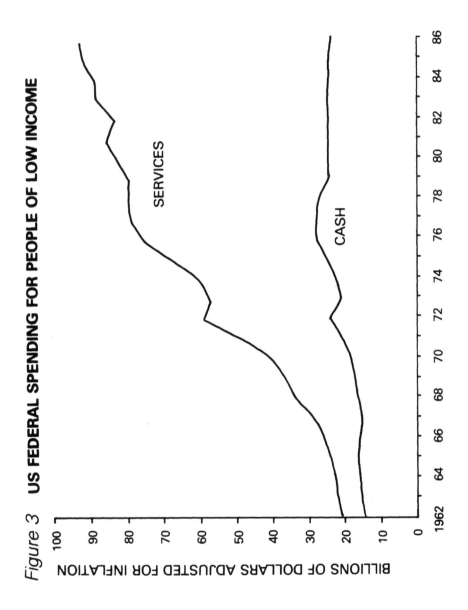

Figure 3 **US FEDERAL SPENDING FOR PEOPLE OF LOW INCOME**

have been one single family below that poverty line in all those years. But what would have happened to social workers, welfare officers, psychiatrists, therapists, economists, planners, etc.? A lot them would have been put out of business, becoming 'les nouveau pauvres'. As one homeless man in Washington, DC noted: 'It would really upset the economy if people were put straight. . . . All those policemen, social workers and blood banks – just think how many people would be unemployed if things got better.'

The Netherlands is an excellent example of all this (DeJong, 1984). In a population of 14.3 million, the labor force is only about 4 million, and almost 1 million people receive some kind of subsidy for purported ailments and handicaps. Most of these, by all indications, are either outright malingering, or the ailment is minor or imaginary. Handicapped people, and/or those that are, or have been made, dependent, are lavishly supported – but by a bewildering array of inefficient provisions and agencies, and there appear to be a number of disincentives to truly independent autonomous living by handicapped people, insofar as all the funding incentives are for handicapped people to live at least in clusters, if not in outright institutions of medium or large size. And the larger the congregation of handicapped people, the more in the way of attendant and nursing care is made available. It is much more difficult to get sufficient attendant service if one lives in open society in ordinary housing. Small community residences with about three to seven residents, and possibly with handicapped and non-handicapped people living together, seem to be very rare. Thus, this system discriminates against independence, communality, and non-congregate and non-institutional living. The largest institution, the internationally renowned Het Dorp, created in the early 1960s, was placed on 100 acres of one of the hilliest locations in the Netherlands, so that the residents' wheelchairs constantly break down, greatly reducing their mobility and independence, and increasing costs.

The controlling interests of PPP societies have good reason to keep the PPP realities hidden, and thus they engage in various forms of deception. A common one in developed countries, including Britain, is to construct the official unemployment figures so as to grossly (virtually fraudulently) understate the true and high rate of unemployment. For instance, official figures generally exclude anyone who has been defined out of the labor force, such as handicapped people, people defined as chronically dependent, unemployed illegal immigrants, retired people who would still like to work, and women who want to work but have had a hard time entering the labor market. In fact, it has been estimated that 58 per cent of European women looking for work were not registered as unemployed.

The PPP realities, as well as the patterns of deception, were dramatically underlined in an analysis of the economic decline of the northern regions of England, and how people – especially young people – are caught in an endless cycle of unemployment: government-subsidised schemes of training for non-existing jobs; training courses on how to get the few jobs that are available – but which would be filled anyway by the plentifully available qualified applicants; short-term government-subsidised employment; and phony so-called 'job clubs' where you talk about your sorry situation, but which lead to employment only for the government-subsidised discussion leaders. The whole thing is one big lie. It appeases a proportion of the unrest, but also socialises young people into a culture of idleness, dependency, anomie, drugs, casual sex, and decadent movements such as punkery and rock. This quite suits the controlling elements, because the decadent classes can at most riot, but they have not the competence and energy to revolutionise.

It is absolutely imperative that we understand that the true but latent function of our human service structure today is not to meet client needs, heal, restore or habilitate, but to employ people so that the wealth gets circulated and the economy keeps 'humming'; to enhance the power, material welfare and other interests of the privileged classes; and to maintain the equilibrium of a mode of societal functioning that rests ultimately on both immoral and invalid assumptions, including those implied in, or strongly associated with, the Keynesian economic model *viz*, unlimited natural resources, unlimited population and economic growth, unlimited technologisation and urbanisation, and the necessity to artificially maintain a certain amount of employment.

That the human service and welfare system is not really designed to diminish the proportion of afflicted and dependent persons is underlined by the fact that this proportion has actually been increasing in recent decades, and this at the very same time that more and more services have been provided, and even yet more grandiose societal and human service aspirations and accomplishments proclaimed.

The unconsciousness that pervades, and indeed even controls, human services is shown in deinstitutionalisation efforts. Such efforts are seen and purveyed as something positive and glorious, a very progressive step – when in actuality the bulk of the scheme turns out to consist merely of different expressions of society's rejection of devalued people. Here, it is important to realise that at least in the United States, a very small proportion – possibly less than 10 per cent – of the deinstitutionalisation effort involves a moral transaction of rehabilitation and community integration. So what is, in effect, merciless dumping of people without genuine supports into abject poverty, slums and ghettoes, into a violent street culture, into other institutions (such as nursing homes), into other hostile, violent, dissocial, asocial or antisocial environments, and into the prison system, is proclaimed as being a beneficent scheme. By such measures, the real intent of society is acted out, namely, to reject, exclude, punish, and even make dead, its handicapped members, but in a disguised – and therefore acceptable – fashion. That the real societal intent is not a positive one is further brought out by the fact that meaningful alternatives to both institutions, and to phony, destructive deinstitutionalisation programs, have been systematically and massively disincentived by law, funding, and administrative fiat.

In this connection, we might also contemplate that in the United States, the criminal justice system assures that there is a permanent overcrowding of prisons, no matter how many are built. For every prisoner or former prisoner who is released or habilitated, the police and the courts not only replace him or her instantly, but add yet more numbers to the prison population. This is exacerbated by the fact that poor, afflicted and oppressed people are currently being redefined as evil and a social menace, and are being transferred from the human service sector into the prison system. Our prison population has doubled in about ten years. One institution after another is being converted into a prison – often with the very same people who once lived there as insane, retarded, epileptic or poor now being called criminal and convict. At Attica alone – one of the highest security prisons in New York State – 200 prisoners were recently reported to be too handicapped to eat properly or unassisted.

All of this is having a devastating impact on everyone involved, but especially on vulnerable classes of people. Rather than benefiting from the bounty of wealth of primary productivity, they are the ones who end up being impressed into clientage, to serve as the unrecognised food on which human service workers, as well as other sectors, enjoy a cannibalistic feast. In a most peculiar fashion, where the laboring child of the English cotton mill was once the food of the economy, an old woman in a nursing home may now be.

Amazingly few people are taking seriously the implications of the trend in the developed world toward a post-primary production society that 'needs' dependent and devalued people in order to provide employment to others. But anyone who fails to understand all this cannot begin to understand what is happening in human services, and that the production and maintenance of devalued people will not only continue, but will also be cleverly disguised, because an honest acknowledgement of the realities is unacceptably unpleasant to most people. We can now see that this chapter might have been entitled'Disability and Dependency: A Creation of Industrial Societies Part II'. I will now add several corollaries or lower-order propositions to all that I have so far discussed.

At least in our type of society, societal policy is largely made by society, by which I mean that most of the time, the real long-term feelings, desires and intents of the majority of people get translated into very real policies.

These very real policies are not necessarily explicitly formulated. For instance, a societal intent to get rid of its old people is not necessarily stated in constitutional, legal, governmental, political party, or other documents, manifestoes, proclamations, etc., but can be nonetheless real and nonetheless rigorously carried out.

Relatedly, programs that carry out a policy may be labeled anything, including the opposite of the policy. Thus, assuring that a dependent class of people remains in a state of dependency may be called rehabilitation or therapy, a place where people die may be called a convalescent hospital, etc. Similarly, since so much of what social systems do is unconscious, it is naive to expect that the official roles, titles, and related verbal labels attached to the transactors of a societal policy will in any way reveal those people's real mission and activity. We should not be surprised if someone who fills a societally sanctioned role of killing people might officially be labeled soldier, police, guard, overseer, leader, servant, saint, social worker, psychologist, psychiatrist, physician, pharmacist, nurse, rehabilitation counselor, barber, milkman, midwife, or what have you. Indeed, the greater the contrast between a societally proclaimed ideal and an actually prevailing policy, the more likely it is that the policy will be surrounded by language that is the opposite of the policy. Thus, major and even controlling policies can be so unconscious and disguised that they are recognised only by a miniscule minority of people within the society.

Once a social policy prevails – and indeed even prior to that point, i.e. when the social policy has attained a near-certain probability of prevailing – there will be no shortage of people who are perfectly willing to carry it out, regardless of what it may be. If the policy is to execute millions, there will be no difficulty finding vast numbers of people who will carry out the executions – especially if, in return for their cooperation, they receive money, prestige or power.

Specifically in regard to most areas of the ever-increasing human services, somewhere over 90 per cent of the people who now work in them either, in my opinion, had no calling to their work in the first place, or they 'died' somewhere along the way – usually within about two years of completing their professional training. People in human service who are 'dead', or who lack a call to service, are prone to commit violence to their clients, especially if these are societally devalued. Thus, on this account alone, there prevails a powerful dynamic toward destructiveness in human service.

Those who clearly recognise a concealed societal policy, especially if that policy is evil and destructive, are confronted by grievous moral choices. As the prophet Ezekiel (33:6) said, those who see the sword coming but fail to sound the alarm are guilty of the blood of the slain. Yet if one pronounces important moral truths that are rejected by most of those around one, one will be successively ridiculed, dismissed, rejected, cast out, persecuted, and even martyred. To the degree that one perceives the important hidden truths and the important overt untruths, proclaims them, and then acts upon what is true and right, one will stand in contradiction to one's world.

And while people who see and proclaim the truth about grave moral issues are persecuted and do come under various attacks, in contrast, those who have been leading, supporting, promoting, and carrying out phony or destructive policies have been, and will continue to be, rewarded.

References

Croxen, M., and Finkelstein, V. (1984) 'Vocational rehabilitation: A USA/UK cross-cultural perspective' *Rehabilitation Literature*, 45, 11–12, pp. 370–374.

DeJong, G. (1984) Independent Living and Disability Policy in the Netherlands: Three Models of Residential Care and Independent Living. Monograph No. 27. New York: World Rehabilitation Fund International Exchange of Experts and Information in Rehabilitation.

Farel, A. M. (1988) 'Choice of priority area by state developmental disabilities councils: Child development as a case example', *Mental Retardation*, 26, 3, pp. 155–159.

Sarason, S. (1969) 'The creation of settings' in Kugel, R., and Wolfensberger W., (Eds) *Changing patterns in residential services for the mentally retarded*, Washington, President's Committee on Mental Retardation, pp. 341–357.

Sarason, S. (1972) *The Creation of settings and the future society*, San Francisco, Jossey Bass.

Chapter Three

Michael Lipsky and Street-Level Bureaucracy: A Neglected Perspective

Bob Hudson

Over the past decade in Britain, there has been renewed political and academic interest in the problem of 'policy implementation'. The concern of a right-wing government to reduce the scale and role of public service bureaucracies has left the air rife with talk of 'value for money', efficiency, effectiveness, performance review and so forth. Policy-makers find themselves under intense pressure to ensure that policy impact reflects the intended direction of change. The broad problem confronting policy-makers is that policy is rarely applied directly to the external world, but is mediated through other institutions and actors. Policy impact is therefore at risk of distortion by these mediators.

In health and welfare agencies, the traditional focus upon the individual has tended to inhibit scrutiny of the collective context within which such activity takes place (Roberts, 1982). Those research studies which have led to theoretical speculation have stemmed mainly from work within industrial organisations, and have tended to see 'implementation deficit' as a problem for top-level policy makers (Hill and Bramley, 1982). Concerns about over-elaborate structures have been a major preoccupation of administrative textbooks for both the public and private sectors and issues about hierarchical control have been the traditional concern of 'management science'. The primary technique for studying behaviour has been the case study.

This is clearly a very limited way of examining social policy implementation. A fresh avenue of inquiry has concentrated upon the behaviour of 'street level' personnel – those actors who do the 'actual' work of the agency – and the ways in which their activities affect the way the public bureaucracy fulfils its public responsibility. In particular, Michael Lipsky (1980) has attempted to synthesise much of the research done in America on the activities of such personnel, and to elaborate a new body of theory on the roles of 'street level bureaucrats'.

Lipsky's analysis has enormous potential for helping us to make sense of the relationship between service providers and service consumers, yet it has had a curiously muted impact. This may be because as Professor of Political Science at Massachusetts Institute of Technology, Lipsky is in the 'wrong' discipline for influencing those studying social welfare. Equally his Goffmanian eclecticism may not appeal to all, for somehow he does manage to address almost every question that occurs to the reader. This chapter will suggest that Lipsky's under-utilised theory has as much significance for understanding welfare service bureaucracies as Goffman's work has had for the understanding of closed institutions.

Lipsky uses the term street level bureaucrat to describe those public service workers who 'interact directly with citizens in the course of their jobs and who have substantial discretion in the execution of their work'. Typical street level workers are teachers, social workers, police officers, doctors, health visitors, certain social security officers, certain housing officers and so forth. It is therefore a notion which encompasses a wide range of welfare services as well as embracing both professionals and non-professionals. By focussing upon this tier of organisational life, Lipsky gets us away from traditional analyses of legislative activity and high ranking policy makers. By attempting to transcend the limitations of case study, he seeks to develop a body of theory on street level activity. He directs our attention to a very large class of people at the sharp end of welfare activity, who routinely behave in ways that remain essentially unexplained.

The essence of Lipsky's case is that street level bureaucrats have enormous power which is scarcely acknowledged in the literature on public administration; that this power extends not only to control over service consumers but also to a considerable autonomy from their employing agency; and that this power is accompanied by the dilemma of working at the sharp end of resource allocation in a situation where demand far exceeds supply. Street level bureaucrats therefore end up making policy in circumstances which are not of their own choosing and which impel them to devise strategies to protect their working environment. In this way, Lipsky is addressing the process whereby zeal is eclipsed and idealism corrupted. It is significant that Lipsky's title refers not to the *power* but to the *dilemma* of the street level bureaucrat.

What is the source of this power? The crucial source is the inescapable exercise of *discretion*. Inescapable, because street level bureaucracies *require* people to make decisions about other people. Indeed, in defence of their activities, organisations will frequently point to the expertise of their members rather than to the success of their endeavours. But once an agency admits that its members have special skills, it also admits to a limitation of the right to define appropriate street level behaviour.

Unlike lower level workers in most organisations, street level bureaucrats have a considerable amount of discretion in determining the nature, amount and quality of benefits and sanctions provided by their agencies. Policemen decide who to arrest and whose behaviour to overlook; teachers make subtle decisions on who is teachable; social workers on who is socially salvageable; health care workers on who has a life worth preserving; housing lettings officers on who get accommodation; social security officers on who gets a community care grant and so on. The discretion is therefore largely brought to bear in the rationing of resources in a situation where demand for them exceeds supply.

Lipsky writes at great length, drawing widely upon evidence, to indicate the techniques used by street level bureaucrats in allocating resources between competing clients. To understand what is taking place, he emphasises the need to take a phenomenological view of street level behaviour – we need to understand the subjective states of mind of the actors. His analysis of the routines developed starts with the proposition that they contribute to control over a difficult and ambiguous work environment. He identifies three broad responses: modification of client demand; modification of job conception; and modification of client conception.

I shall look very briefly at each of these, but this does not do justice to the richness of Lipsky's analysis of modification of client demand. Although street level bureaucrats can rarely charge for their services, most other forms of demand control are open to them, such as perpetuating delay, witholding information, and stigmatising the process of service delivery. Social policy has yet to address this field effectively at an empirical level.

If necessary, street level bureaucrats can simply *control* clients, or at least obtain their cooperation with client processing procedures. Several aspects of practice contribute to the routine control of clients. First, street level bureaucrats interact with clients in settings that symbolise and limit their relationship – this may encompass such matters as uniforms, location, and the content, timing and pace of interaction. Second, clients are isolated from one another, and are therefore more likely to see themselves as responsible for their situations – indeed street level bureaucrats will tend to resist client organisation when it arises. Third, the procedures and services of street level bureaucrats are presented as benign and always in the best interests of clients.

But street level bureaucrats do not simply deal with occupational hazards by limiting client demand. They also modify their *own* activities and perceptions of their jobs and clients. Modification of job conception basically means that street level bureaucrats modify their objectives to match better their ability to perform. Lipsky gives several examples. One is 'psychological withdrawal', resulting in a workforce relatively unbothered by the discrepancy between what they are *supposed* to do and what they *actually* do. By accepting limitations as fixed rather than problematic, innovation is discouraged and mediocrity encouraged. It is a situation not unfrequently chronicled in research into the functioning of long stay psychiatric and subnormality hospitals.

Modification of client conception is even more subtle. Lipsky argues that street level bureaucrats who are unable to provide all clients with their best efforts, develop conceptual mechanisms to divide up the client population and rationalise the division, even though the consequence of this may be at variance with the formal goals of the organisation. This may involve 'creaming off' those clients who seem most likely to succeed in terms of bureaucratic success criteria; or it may simply involve differentiating between those clients deemed to be deserving and undeserving.

Even with this brief review, I hope to have conveyed something of the power exercised by the street level bureaucrat. But to what extent can the street level bureaucrat act autonomously of the employing agency? Lipsky himself argues that accountability to the organisation is virtually impossible to achieve where street level bureaucrats exercise a high degree of discretion. I shall return to the issue of accountability shortly, but for now it is worth re-emphasising that street level bureaucrats do carry out much of the difficult rationing at client level, and it is therefore often convenient for organisations to permit this discretion to continue relatively unabated. The exercise of street level bureaucrat discretion can be functional to the organisation.

Lipsky's analysis is useful for helping us to understand a wide range of public welfare activities, including services for people with a disability. Disappointingly little attempt has been made, in any field of activity, to put Lipsky's ideas to the test. I shall look briefly at some areas of provision for people with a disability which could benefit from Lipsky's work and which do at least have some data on the activities of street level bureaucrats.

First, Special Educational Needs. In the USA an attempt has been made by one of Lipsky's associates, Richard Weatherley (1977), to apply the street level perspective to the study of the implementation of special education reform in Massachusetts, where the Comprehensive Special Education Law introduced provisions very similar to those in Britain's 1981 Education Act. Schools were required to operate much more sophisticated procedures for assessing needs and for developing individualised programmes for children, and, as in Britain, were expected to do this without significantly more resources. Weatherley shows how the realities at street level constrained and distorted the reforms hoped for by state legislators – assessments were not conducted; limits were placed on the number of assessments held; assessment schedules were biased in favour of children likely to be inexpensive; parental deference to professional authority was sought, and so forth. In short, street level bureaucrats sought to secure their work environment.

In Britain, no attempt to apply Lipsky's theory explicitly has been made, but in her study of 'statementing' under the 1981 Education Act, Nicki Cornwell (1987) does reveal some telling detail about the *modus operandi* of street level bureaucrats, which can help us to explain the wide variation in the percentage of school populations with statements. I shall take only two of her many illustrations, the first in relation to modifying demand by reducing service levels. In the London Borough she studied, she found that although administrators had to follow the advice of psychologists about placement, somehow demand and supply had to match. She writes that: 'Some negotiation might be needed with psychologists about this, and a gentleman's agreement reached about not putting the borough in an embarrassing situation.' Again, on modification of job conception, she argues that statementing amounts to little more than a continuously loaded conveyor belt in which decisions on outcomes are made as soon as the child is referred for assessment, but it is important in order to keep up the appearance of open and rational decision making. This is not only for the purpose of legality, but also for the psychological well being of the street level bureaucrats involved. She writes: 'The appearance of negotiation can help to obscure the reality of the situation from the professionals involved, who can remain convinced that they are taking part in a rational assessment.'

In the field of social work Carol Satyamurti (1981) has written tellingly of the adoption of stereotyped responses to clients. She argues:

> In the social work literature, the client is often spoken of as though he were a fully consenting adult participant in the social work relationship. In practice, however, it often seemed that a parent-child relationship was a more powerful model, as far as the social worker was concerned, for her dealings with clients. This was true both at the level of face-to-face encounters, and at the level of decision-making affecting the client.

As illustrations of this, Satyamurti cites the way in which social workers encouraged dependent behaviour in their clients, the way in which social workers treated appointments and called without warning on clients, the terms in which social workers discussed clients and the assumptions they made about client 'irresponsibility'.

A third area which could usefully draw upon Lipsky's work is that of income maintenance policies, which affords a useful example of street level bureaucrats who do not hold professional status. Folk-lore is rich with tales of encounters between social security officers and claimants, but research is at a premium. An important exception is Cooper's (1985) detailed consideration of the former supplementary benefit scheme at a range of offices.

Much of Lipsky's theory is reflected in Cooper's findings. The impact of unmanageable demand is evident. He writes: 'In most offices, most of the time, the emphasis was on getting the work done at all, rather than on doing it well. . . . Many of the difficulties found in relationships between staff and claimants could be interpreted in part as devices used by staff for controlling the amount of work with which they were required to cope.' In the pursuit of coping practices, relatively junior staff were left pretty much to their own devices, but it is clear that much of this is delegated autonomy which it is functional for the organisation to permit. He notes: 'In keeping with the emphasis on "getting the work done", it was apparent on several occasions that the calibre of junior staff was judged by their ability to dispose of cases rapidly and without follow-up work, with scant reference to the outcome for claimants.'

One of the prime coping mechanisms described by Cooper is illustrative of Lipsky's notion of modification of client conception. Treatment of claimants was found to vary according to a judgement made about them by officers on the basis of very little information and a brief acquaintance. People with a disability tend to emerge from these encounters better than most, but sympathy is hardly the stuff of citizenship. Cooper's vignettes are illuminating. I shall take two contrasting examples, both dealt with by the same officer.

> . . . a married man in his 50's who had been out of work for a number of years owing to a chronic chest condition. He had called to drop in his latest medical certificate and to put a general enquiry about extra help with fuel costs over the winter. Mike (the officer) treated him very decently, asking after his and his wife's welfare, and thanking him pleasantly for the certificate. He then gave an outline of help available for fuel costs and passed over the relevant leaflet, saying, 'This will tell you how to apply. The form is on the back, see? If you have any doubts or queries come back in and we'll sort it out, OK?'

The next caller was less fortunate:

. . . there followed Mr. Z., a young Pakistani who had recently been made redundant, bringing in his rent book and last three wage slips. He appeared shy and confused in the office environment. Mike's approach was abrupt. He wanted to know why Mr. Z. had come in. Mr. Z. said he had been told to bring the documents. 'You must have heard wrong,' said Mike. 'We tell people to post them in. Why don't you leave it with the man on reception?' Mike took the papers and dismissed Mr. Z., with the words 'Right enough, we'll keep these and you'll get them back sometime in the post. There was nothing else was there?' As Mr. Z. retires, evidently disconcerted, Mike remarked 'What do you make of that one? Bloody odd. The best thing you can do is get them in and get them out when they're like him. We get quite a few Pakis like that, wandering in like lost sheep.'

It is worth emphasising that Cooper is describing the implementation of the 1980 Social Security Act which ostensibly afforded claimants legal entitlement to benefits. The 1986 Social Security Act has largely replaced entitlement with discretion and will make the street level bureaucrat claimant relationship even more one-sided. The first set of figures on the community care grant, for example, reveal that six of the London DHSS offices spent none of their budget, and elsewhere the variation is huge.

If Lipsky's analysis has validity, then concern about the accountability of street level bureaucrats is bound to be high, for accountability is the link between bureaucracy and democracy. Lipsky himself argues that such accountability is virtually impossible to achieve where workers exercise a high degree of discretion, and since he also takes the view that discretion itself is inescapable, the likelihood of securing accountability seems slim.

This pessimistic appraisal has not diminished the zeal with which various forms of accountability are pursued. Four main types can be distinguished: accountability to the organisation; accountability to consumers; accountability to the law; and accountability to professional norms. Each is problematic.

Accountability to the Organisation

Attempts to increase accountability to the organisation through administrative controls (both sanctions and incentives) is the most common effort to increase congruence between worker behaviour and agency policy. But for the street level bureaucrat, the formal rewards of agencies are likely to play only a minor role in directing behaviour.

Prottas (1978) points out that in many public service bureaucracies, the turnover of street level bureaucrats is very high, therefore the relevance of promotions, salary increases and retirement benefits is correspondingly low. The same is true when the street level bureaucrats are established professionals, as in law and medicine, and have other career alternatives.

It is, in any case, difficult for the agency to decide when it is appropriate to deploy such controls as it has available. Street level bureaucrat performance is notoriously difficult to define and measure, and much of the performance occurs in places inaccessible to supervisors. Greater demands can be made for written records to serve as an independent check, but when matters are ambiguous, they are less than useful; they either support the decision of the street level bureaucrat or do not mention it. Indeed, Prottas (1978) suggests that: 'The most striking characteristic of client files in many public bureaucracies is their sparseness'.

Organisational measures to *increase* scrutiny of street level activity are strewn with difficulty. Conceivably, someone could replicate the street level bureaucrat's interaction with clients, but this is a desperate measure, of use in inhibiting flagrant abuses, but not a practical means of assuring routine compliance. Similarly, close supervision will be resisted. Alvin Gouldner (1964) showed clearly that all workers have an idea of what constitutes normal supervision, and any attempt to exceed that norm will be identified as 'close supervision'.

Downs (1966) called it a 'law' of organisational behaviour, that 'the greater the efforts made to control subordinated officials, the greater the efforts by those subordinates to evade or counteract such control'. This is borne out by the discussion by Fox (1974) on the relationship between rule-imposition and low-trust relationships. Coming from a concern with industrial relations, he shows how a 'top-down' concern with detailed prescription, creates and reinforces low-trust relationships. Subordinates therefore feel little commitment, which results in an even further tightening of control, and a further diminution of commitment. Hill and Bramley (1986) note: 'Low motivation in a rule-bound context produces restriction of output, working to rule, industrial sabotage and strikes. In public administration, there is often another person or member of the public, rather than a machine, to feel the effects of low official morale.'

Accountability to Consumers

Proposals for greater client autonomy tend to suffer from the fact that clients generally remain relatively powerless, but there nevertheless remains a *potential* for contributing to changing street level relationships. There are two main variants.

One approach is to attempt to *eliminate street-level workers as buffers* between government and citizens. A class of proposals utilising such an approach is represented by the voucher system, which promises to import consumer sovereignty into the production of welfare services. In Britain, two recent major reports have come out in favour of vouchers – the Griffiths Report on Community Care (1988) and the Wagner Report on Residential Care (1988).

The debate is a complex one, but it will be very difficult to establish the conditions under which consumers of services are fully informed about the wide variety of options, and it is therefore difficult to create the rudiments of competition upon which the theory depends. Given Lipsky's argument that *agencies* find it difficult to assess the appropriateness of street level behaviour, it would clearly be difficult for *clients* to assess the appropriateness of a service.

An alternative route to consumer sovereignty is to *eliminate public workers from service contexts*, which, with proper support, might be handled by citizens with little assistance. Advocacy, and particularly self-advocacy, would fit into this route, and this represents one of the more exciting developments relating to people with disabilities. But at this stage, it would not be wise to making anything other than provisional claims for the success of such experiments. It has to be remembered that while clients seek services and benefits, street level bureaucrats seek control over the process of providing them, and they will not easily relinquish their grip.

A further possibility, and an increasingly fashionable one, is to democratise through forms of participation close to service delivery level – decentralisation. In social work in Britain, such notions have become increasingly popular since the Barclay Report (1982), but again, claims can be little more than provisional. In terms of Lipsky's analysis, if decentralisation intensifies pressure upon street level bureaucrats by making them more accessible, then they will develop new strategies for protecting themselves.

Accountability to the Law

Judicial processes might be used to secure 'rights' to public benefits and services. Legal philosophers such as Dicey (1905), saw the growth of the 'collective state' as a threat to liberty, and the intervention of the judiciary as a brake upon the state. However, not only are procedures inaccessible to underprivileged citizens, but the legal system is not well-equipped to deal with the problems associated with the exercise of discretion by street level bureaucrats.

Rather closer to organisational level, clients can bring information to the attention of other members of the bureaucracy. The ubiquity of appeals procedures in many welfare bureaucracies testifies to the hope that the availability of this channel will increase the compliance of street level bureaucrats. However, we still know relatively little about the actual uses to which appeals procedures are put, and about their effects upon street level behaviour.

Lipsky, with characteristic scepticism, argues that from the street level perspective, appeals procedures should exhibit three qualities. First, it must look as though the channels are open. Second, the channels must be costly to use, rarely successful and (if successful) not well publicised. Third, a single client should not be able to gain redress for a class of clients. This does seem to encompass much tribunal and appeal activity in Britain.

Accountability to Professional Norms

Lipsky concludes that most street level work is not open to meaningful revision by limiting discretion, removing public employees from interaction with clients, or modestly altering the bureaucratic structure. He stresses the idealism and commitment of many practitioners, but sees this idealism undermined by work situations and organisation structures.

In his concluding chapter, he seems to opt for the enhancement of professionalism as a way of coping with the problems of street level bureaucracy. The argument, he says, '. . . comes down simply to the realisation that control of occupational groups must come from within group members'. This is perhaps a rather insipid up-shot, particularly since he also recognises that: 'The problem with the "professional fix" lies in the gap between the service orientations of professionals in theory and in practice'.

Hill and Bramley (1986) take the view that '. . . it is far from certain that professional monopolies are not greater evils than the forms of discretion and "street level" behaviour they profess to bring under control'. This is broadly in line with Wilding's (1982) review of professional power, which concluded: 'Professional self-regulation is unsatisfactory. No profession has shown anything but the most lukewarm interest in monitoring and maintaining the standard of work of its members . . . There is little or no acceptance of a consumer's right to comment on, or complain about, the substance of the service offered'.

The Intractability of the Street-Level Bureaucrat

There would therefore seem to be clear limits on the extent to which the freedom of action of front-line staff can be circumscribed. Lipsky argues that a bureaucratic accountability *policy* should possess four prerequisites. First, agencies must know what they want workers to do; where objectives are multiple and conflicting, agencies must be able to rank their preferences. Second, agencies must know how to measure workers' performances. Third, agencies must be able to compare workers with one another, to establish a standard for judgment. And finally, agencies must have incentives and sanctions capable of disciplining workers.

These preconditions tend *not* to apply to street level bureaucrats, because street level bureaucracies *require* people to make decisions about other people. To say that human interaction is required in service delivery, is to suggest that the situation requires judgments to be made about potentially ambiguous situations; the requisite human judgment simply cannot be programmed.

Hill (1982) reminds us that many examples of deviation from the apparent intentions of policy can be seen as situations in which the centre has no real concern that its policy should become manifest. There is a degree of 'sanctioned unaccountability'. As Hill puts it: 'Delegation may owe more to a desire to obscure political responsibility, than to an acceptance of the need to come to terms with street level bureaucracy'. It would seem that the best that can be managed is a little reining in here and a little wing clipping there.

Changing Street-Level Behaviour: The Wider Context

Ultimately, the contradictory tendencies in street level bureaucracies cannot be understood without examining their role in society, and the way in which society impinges upon the character of bureaucratic relations. The main danger of Lipsky's phenomenological approach is that it can be construed as a form of ideological relativism, largely ignoring the question of *why* one 'weltanschauung' is considered more legitimate than another. Such studies usually operate at a level of analysis which is divorced from any notion of power in social relations.

Although Lipsky does not systematically attempt to link his analysis to a broader perspective, he does point us in that direction. The influence of the wider context is raised at two levels. First, that the character of client treatment at the hands of street level bureaucrats, reflects and reinforces class and ethnic divisions. The extent to which the clients are prepared for the impersonalism, hierarchy and institutionalisation of bureaucracy, is also a reflection of such divisions.

But he also goes beyond this, in raising an even more fundamental question – in what ways do street level bureaucracies reflect and perpetuate the values of the larger society? An adequate analysis of the actual exercise of discretion at 'face to face' level must be informed by an understanding of the structural position of welfare institutions and their relationship to the broader social, political and economic framework of society. Novak (1988) makes some attempt to do this in his Marxist interpretation of relief of poverty by the state, but overall there has been little attempt to connect and reconcile micro- and macro-sociological concerns.

The poorer people are, the greater the power that street level bureaucracies have over them. In the 1960s and 1970s, a typical government response to social problems was to commission a corps of street level bureaucrats to attend to them, for as Lipsky notes, '. . . it is easier to develop employment for street level bureaucrats, than to reduce income inequalities'. It is through street level bureaucracies that society organises the control, restriction and maintenance of relatively powerless groups.

Despite his focus upon intra-organisational processes, Lipsky nevertheless concludes: '. . . the reconstruction of street level bureaucracies in unlikely to take place in the absence of a broad movement for social and economic justice. . . . Isolated reform efforts cannot plausibly be expected to bear the full weight of social change'. This is not a message in mood with the political spirit of the 1980s, in Britain or the USA. It may help to explain the relative neglect of Lipsky's analysis.

What, then, is the message to come out of Lipsky? It is not that street level bureaucrats are simply malicious and cunning functionaries interested only in their own comfort. Rather, it is that in looking at the dilemmas in their working day, we can see just how problematic a role they are asked to play in the policy making system. Academically, the pressing need is to find out more about how street level bureaucrats are actually behaving. Getting at the truth would be problematic, but must be confronted. If we wish to understand policy implementation, we must understand the street level bureaucrat.

My thanks to Professor Michael Hill, Department of Social Policy, University of Newcastle-upon-Tyne, England, for his help with this article.

References

Barclay Report (1982) *Social Workers: Their Role and Tasks*, Bedford Square Press.
Cooper, S. (1985) *Observation in Supplementary Benefit Offices*, Supplementary Benefit Working Paper C, Policy Studies Institute.
Cornwell, N. (1987) *Statementing and the 1981 Education Act*, Cranfield Press.
Dicey, A. V. (1905) *Lectures on the Relation Between Law and Public Opinion in England*, Macmillan.
Downs, A. (1966) *Inside Bureaucracy*, Boston, Little, Brown.
Fox, A. (1974) *Beyond Contract: Work, Power and Trust Relations*, Faber.
Gouldner, A. (1964) *Patterns of Industrial Bureaucracy*, New York, Free Press.
Griffiths Report (1988) *Community Care: An Agenda for Action*, HMSO.
Hill, M. (1982) 'Street Level Bureaucracy in Social Work and Social Services Departments', *Research Highlights*, 4, University of Aberdeen.
Hill, M. and Bramley, G. (1986) *Analysing Social Policy*, Basil Blackwell.
Lipsky, M. (1980) *Street Level Bureaucracy: Dilemmas of the Individual in Public Services*, Russell Sage Foundation.
Novak, T. (1988) *Poverty and the State*, Open University Press.
Prottas, J. D. (1978) 'The Power of the Street Level Bureaucrat in Public Service Bureaucracies', *Urban Affairs Quarterly*, 13, 3.
Roberts, E. (1982) 'A Presentation of Perspectives of Organisational Theory Relevant to Social Work', *Research Highlights*, 4, University of Aberdeen.
Satyamurti, C. (1981) *Occupational Survival*, Blackwell.
Wagner Report (1988) *Residential Care: A Positive Choice*, HMSO.
Weatherley, R. and Lipsky, M. (1977), 'Street Level Bureaucrats and Institutional Innovation: Implementing Special Education Reform', *Harvard Education Review*, 47, pp. 171–197.
Wilding, P. (1982) *Professional Power and Social Welfare*, Routledge and Kegan Paul.

Chapter Four

Disabled People, Normality and Social Work

Paul Abberley

Whilst it is my contention that an historically and socially constructed category of 'disabled people' experience, as members of that category, a common oppression, it is also true that the modes in which that oppression are experienced vary in relation to a number of factors, one of which is the nature of their disability. The illustrations and examples employed in this chapter relate most directly to individuals with motor impairments who embody the most commonly held stereotypes of disabled people, and indeed 'stand for' disabled people in the 'disabled' logo to be found in parking spaces and public lavatories. It should not however be assumed that all disabled people experience their oppression in the forms outlined here, nor that people who do not experience these particular forms of oppression are therefore not disabled. For such sections of the social category 'disabled people' such as deaf people, blind people, mentally handicapped people, different constraints operate, and these require separate and detailed analysis if we are not ourselves to fall into the trap of the social stereotyping of disabled people. The recognition of this should be seen as greatly strengthening my case as to the inadequacy of social work education in relation to the needs of disabled people.

A frequently voiced wish of disabled people is the desire to be regarded as normal. For relatively mobile but visibly impaired people, a lifetime of being stared at, 'strained interaction', as described by Katz *et al* (1979) and management of stigma as documented by interactionist researchers like Davis (1961) and Goffman (1963) can become wearing, to say the least. Indeed, combined with other features of social disadvantage and physiologically based problems it can result in what some have termed 'cripples battle-fatigue'.

It is not surprising, then, that many disabled people welcome the ostensibly progressive assertions of those, disabled or not, that disabled people are 'really' normal. Indeed writers on disability as far apart in other respects as Goffman (1963) and Sutherland (1981) assert the essential normality of disabled people, though for diametrically opposed reasons. Goffman argues that the deviance from which stigmatisation results is the product of social values, not of a physical reality, whilst Sutherland, noting that there are things that any individual cannot do and that, disabled or not, we all grow old, and with age experience reductions in certain capacities, concludes 'disablement is not merely the physical state of a small minority of people. It is the normal condition of humanity' (p. 18).

What unites these two very different writers on disability is this, then: they think disabled people are 'really' normal. From both positions it follows then that the supposed abnormality of disabled people is the result of some kind of 'mistake'; if only people would/could think about things differently, change their 'attitudes' they would recognise that we're REALLY the same as them, we're NORMAL after all. The problem, then, is all in the mind, and the best way to deal with it is to assert, as loudly and as often as possible, the normality of disabled people. (The fact that Goffman's analysis implies that the overcoming of stigma is in all probability impossible is not the point at issue here).

However, as a disabled person and a sociologist whose working life is in considerable part spent in teaching non-disabled students on health and welfare courses about disability, I wish to argue that such a view is not only profoundly mistaken as to the source and nature of the multiple disadvantages experienced by disabled people, but that its propagation, in the context of modern Britain, serves not to combat but to perpetuate the oppression of disabled people.

What is required by disabled people today is not to have people going round proclaiming how we're really like everyone else, but rather the repeated and detailed documentation of the quantitative and qualitative aspects of difference between the lives of disabled and non-disabled people, coupled with the development of theoretical accounts of how and why this happens, which are directed towards change.

What we need is the development, by and for disabled people, of something analogous to a feminist perspective, which at the same time as asserting and stressing real differences, combats false and oppressive explanations of the origin and nature of those differences. We need a theory and a practice which sees the fundamental problem of disabled people as one of oppression (see Abberley, 1987, for a fuller account of this).

The Origins and Nature of Professional Knowledge

How does this relate to ideas about the normality or otherwise of disabled people?

The first point to note is that whilst in principle anyone can define normality in any way they want, only certain definitions 'stick'. Definitions with 'stickability' tend to be those produced by groups with power. The most powerful definitions of normality in terms of their effects upon those to whom they are applied are, for disabled people, those propagated and perpetuated by those with the most wideranging and immediate power over us, namely the medical and welfare professions.

Whilst a variety of studies have been carried out which detail historical analyses of the relationship between 'social' and 'scientific' factors in relation to medicine, there is little work of this kind in relation to welfare provision for physically disabled people, and certainly nothing to compare in theoretical and empirical richness to social constructionist accounts of madness to be found in the work of, for example, Foucault (1967) and Scull (1979, 1984). Nevertheless, what we can learn from this work is that, in relation to disability too, concepts of normality are developed as both a product and condition of medical and welfare systems.

As such, notions and implications of judgments about normality will vary in relation to the organisation of care delivery systems and their associated ideologies of welfare and medical practice.

Whilst, in general, services for younger disabled adults in Britain have been described by one writer as 'the worst in Europe' (Gloag, 1984), another feature, which has most recently been pointed out by Beardshaw (1988, 37) is that 'services for disabled people have been repeatedly – and aptly – likened to the maze at Hampton Court'.

It is my purpose in this chapter to consider just one strand of provision, or lack of it, that which is associated with social services departments and social workers. Various recent studies (Thomas *et al*, 1985; Hirst, 1985; Owens, 1987) indicate dissatisfaction amongst disabled clients with the attention they receive from social workers. In part this results from the tendency of social services departments to concentrate their more experienced and senior staff, who have lighter caseloads, in work with families, relegating disabled clients to the care of junior, less experienced practitioners (Challis and Ferlie, 1988). But I think it is as much a product of the knowledge, or, perhaps more accurately, lack of knowledge, that social workers have of disabled people, and it is this that I will go on to address.

As far as traditional social work is concerned, in general, lack of 'normality' is perceived in those social groups which are the objects of welfare provision, and are by definition not 'normal' except insofar as they share in the 'normal abnormality' of needing care, protection, assistance and constraint, which is held in common by all the diverse recipients of welfare.

Satyamurti (1981) has argued that social workers traditionally see their clients as unreliable, helpless and unable to plan. Thus to see the disabled person as a 'normal' client is to ascribe to her the very characteristics possessed by clients in general which are also identified with disability. So, traditional social work sees disabled people as sharing in the 'normal abnormality' ascribed to all its clients.

This traditional approach drew for its theoretical basis upon positivistic accounts of deviant client groups, perceived in terms of their individual or collective pathology. The academic component of the training of social workers under such a system consisted, in crude terms, in familiarising her with theoretically based recipes for action with the specific client groups with whom she would work.

Owen, in a survey of social work literature and interviews with disabled people who have undertaken Masters programmes in social work in the United States, concludes that teaching and the literature upon which it is based seriously misrepresents the situation of disabled clients. Specifically, he states that:

> The view of disability revealed by social work literature emphasises three myths:
> 1 Disability is primarily a problem of the very young and the very old. The 'normal' family members can be given some assistance in dealing with their relatives' 'affliction'. This is a proper role for the profession.
> 2 The disfunctions (sic) of the middle years are primarily emotional or mental difficulties. The medical model is appropriate in dealing with such individuals.
> 3 Because there apparently are few disabled individuals of working age who might need social services, there is little need to establish new models of service to address this population.
>
> (Owen, 1985, 400)

As far as Britain is concerned, this finding is echoed in the Royal College of Physicians Report (1986) that provision for people of working age is the least adequate aspect of services for disabled people.

A 'myth' is not a 'mere' fiction. Rather it is an 'explanatory fiction' which serves to define, explain and justify a particular set of social arrangements and concerns. So, the traditional Social Work Myth, in Britain and the United States, has the effect of excluding a whole band of disabled people from view. This 'knowledge' of disabled people, as of any other client group, does not exist separate from modes of social work practice, and even though the development of theory and practice may well procede in an uneven manner, there is a long-running tendency towards a correspondence between the two.

But, it will be objected, social work practice and education today is very different from this traditional model; surely changes are taking place which are fast making social work more responsive to the real needs of disabled people? Doesn't new, progressive, 'radical' social work see, and provide for, disabled people of working age?

I would argue, however, that during the last 20 years the particular structural changes which have taken place in social work in Britain have had the effect of producing a new but equally damaging 'myth' about disabled people, namely that they are 'normal'.

Genericism

The 'genericisation' of social work, following the Seerbohm report of 1968, was expressly aimed at solving the organisational problems of a multiplicity of discrete agencies involved in fragmentary work with a client by creating the omnicompetent social worker.

But along with this organisational change went an ideological transformation, which contained profound implications for the theoretical basis of social work practice:

> We see our proposals not simply in terms of organisation but as embodying a wider conception of social services, directed to the well-being of the whole community and not only of social casualties, and seeing the community it serves as the basis of its authority, resources and effectiveness
>
> (Seerbohm, 1968, para 474).

Subsequent reviews, by Barclay in 1982 and Griffiths in 1988, have continued and made more explicit this trend, which, broadly speaking, shifts the focus of social work from individual clients to client groups, and presents social workers as 'upholders of networks' who 'enable, empower, support and encourage social networks'.

Because of this social and community orientation, genericisation leads to an increased significance for such academic disciplines as Social Policy and Sociology as the theoretical basis for social work practice. Now the focus becomes rather different, for, as I have argued elsewhere (1987), the predominant focus of literature in this area is with disabled people of working age.

This emphasis performs important functions for the present social system. Firstly, by directing attention away from impairment associated with ageing, it naturalises this aspect of the situation, and reduces the amount of perceived disability in society, so that disability appears as 'exceptional'.

Secondly, it concentrates on that aspect of disability, namely its ability to effect potential workers, which is the primary concern of capitalism, for which the 'problem' of disability is why these people aren't productive, how to return them to productivity, and, if this is not seen as economically viable, how to handle their non-productivity in a manner which causes as little disruption as possible to the over-riding imperatives of capital accumulation and the maximisation of profits. Yet if the primary object of such theories is the 'young' disabled, their effects reverberate far beyond their immediate subjects. One effect of the downgrading of the disabled state is to lead all people, including the 'young' disabled themselves, to deny their own suffering and to normalize their situation, thus maintaining the existing structures of social organisation and of work. Beyond this, society as a whole is affected, via the propagation of the work ethic and notions of normalcy and masculinity implicitly contained in such theories. At this level there is a parallel with the argument (Brittan and Maynard, 1984) that racial and sexual oppression are integrally connected to masculine power, in the notion of masculinity as mastery over nature. The points raised by Hunt (1966, 146), who argues that disabled people challenge the prevailing norms of society in five main ways, 'as unfortunate, useless, different, oppressed and sick', indicate how the mode of being of disabled people can be seen as constituting a negation of masculinity as thus conceived.

So, I would argue that the changes in social work organisation and practice which have occurred in the last twenty years have concomitant changes in the theoretical basis of that practice. These changes have brought the concerns of social work more in line with the interests of the state as far as disability is concerned.

'Radical' Social Work

This transformation of the role and the theoretical basis of social work did not, however, take place in a social vacuum. Representatives of various client-groups, in particular the women's and anti-racist movements, have fought for an increased say in the amount and kind of service provided.

Social work's response to this has been to develop 'radical' alternatives to traditional social work which seek to erode the distinction between practitioner and client, and to demolish the hierarchical structure of the relationship. They stress a continuity between practitioner and client, and thus the 'normality' of the latter.

But for disabled people this runs into a problem (as it does in a more publicly acknowledged way for black people): in the absence of any significant number of disabled social workers, the experiential basis for this can only be a tentative and dubious identification, based on partial and fragmentary simulations and appercus.

To take a common example: in training, potential practitioners are often encouraged to play about in wheelchairs to promote 'identification', and on the basis of this new 'knowledge' to assert their common humanity with their disabled clients. Now I am not suggesting that such practices do not contain positive features. But problems can be produced by such activities.

Firstly, there is the danger that the full nature and extent of the difference between the lives of disabled and 'normal' people is underestimated, and that too facile an 'identification' with disabled people is produced, so that students conclude the exercise feeling, for example, that a chairbound person is just an able bodied social worker on wheels instead of legs. Such exercises can have the effect of 'marginalising' the significance of disability through a spurious and superficial empathy.

Even as far as physical difficulties are concerned, the identification may be an illusory one. The difficulty of propelling a wheel chair, to take one common example from experiential learning programmes, is in fact far greater for a novice than for someone whose shoulders are adapted through a lifetime's practice. It is also the case that the major problems experienced by chair-bound people are often to do with pain, or lack of sensation, or incontinence, rather than mobility, and simulation exercises necessarily fail to address these.

Autobiographical accounts of sudden disablement (e.g. Sacks, 1984, Murphy, 1987) share as a perennial feature a sense of shock at the failure of anything in the author's previous experience to prepare them for the disabled state. Such evidence would seem to indicate a severely limited value for simulation exercise.

A way round this might of course be to get students to read these books. However, one consequence of the prevalence of such literature, and its consumption by non-disabled professionals, is a particular kind of account of disability, a kind of asociological romanticism which presents disabled people as carrying out some doomed and lonely symbolic struggle on behalf of humankind as a whole against the intransigence of nature.

This view of the cripple as hero is even found on occasion in the work of the better writers on disability (e.g. Shearer, 1986).

To say this is to break away from the dominant approaches in psychology in the first half of this century, summarised by Kammerer (1940) as follows:

> Although there is agreement that personality maladjustment results from crippling, there are essentially two points of view as to how it actually occurs. The first seems to assume that the presence of any sort of crippling or physical handicap is sufficient in itself to occasion the development of personality disorder. The second viewpoint maintains that in cases of personality maladjustment, the crippled child has been subject to unwise family influences.

Some writers have rightly rejected these kinds of psychological accounts and their more modern variant, 'mourning theory', as both empirically unsupportable, and unacceptable in their consequences (see Oliver, 1983). But in doing so they have put nothing in its place, and have thus done little to develop a psychology of disabled people FOR disabled people, beyond the albeit necessary critique of oppressive approaches. In its absence, the non-scientific, romantic stance of heroicism holds sway as 'the alternative'.

Such 'heroicism', whilst superficially a more attractive role, is in the long run not an advance for disabled people, since it obscures the social origins of the oppression of disabled people, and encourages the masking of psychological suffering.

We may usefully draw an analogy here with the women's movement, where, for a period, the heroic stance – 'women are powerful' – stood as a rejection of the multifarious sexist psychologies, and accounts based in labelling theory suggested that no 'real' psychological differences between the sexes existed in a society increasingly seen to be founded upon sexual oppression. From here, however, it soon became apparent that if the real extent and nature of sexual oppression were to be understood, and services appropriate to real needs struggled for, feminist psychologies which recognised the individual consequences of collective oppression, and traced their causes beyond the individual to the mechanisms of that oppression, would have to be developed.

Indeed, it would be surprising if the institutionalised inequality produced by social definitions did not exact a psychological price from subordinated groups. Carmen *et al* (1981) argue:

> Since men hold the power and authority, women are rewarded for developing a set of psychological characteristics that accommodate

to and please men. Such traits – submissiveness, compliance, passivity, helplessness, weakness – have been encouraged in women and incorporated into some prevalent psychological theories in which they are defined as innate or inevitable characteristics of women. However, they are more accurately conceptualised as learned behaviours by which all subordinate group members attempt to ensure their survival . . . behaviours such as inhibition, passivity and submissiveness do not lead to favourable outcomes and play a role in the development of psychological problems.

Similar points must be made in relation to disabled people, and are already empirically supported by the plethora of data gathered by such interactionist researchers as Goffman and Davis.

Disabled people do not need to deny the individual psychological costs they pay, rather they need to identify them as a most directly experienced aspect of oppression, and dispute not the existence of psychological distress in disabled people but the kinds of causal account that are produced. To do this we need to break away from the comforting myth of heroicism, which is equally part of our oppression.

As far as non-disabled social workers are concerned, I am suggesting, then, that the project of 'empathetic understanding' has severe limitations, not only in terms of practicality, but also in its theoretical basis, which assumes too great a continuity of experience between disabled and non-disabled people – in a word, an inappropriate 'normality'.

Benefit Abnormality

I have argued that with genericisation the theoretical basis of social work practice resides increasingly in the academic areas of sociology and social policy. We now confront another danger involved in the assertion of normality: that it avoids any consideration of the particular structural determinants of the disadvantages of disabled people. I will go on to look at some of the most topical of these.

A consideration of the implications of the Social Security 'Reforms' of April 1988 (NACAB, 1988; Turner and Kepley, 1988) for disabled people indicates how regarding disabled people as 'normal' results in a substantial increase in disadvantage.

Under the previous system of benefits, unemployed disabled people could claim social security at a higher rate, and were also eligible for a number of Additional Requirement Payments to meet such needs as extra laundry expenses, special dietary requirements, extra heating, wear and tear on clothing etc., which were a consequence of specific disabilities. For all its deficiencies and inadequacies, this system recognised that, in principle, the needs of disabled people are often different from those of the 'normal' claimant.

Under the new Social Fund, the higher long-term benefit rate is abolished and the ARPs replaced by flat rate premiums, which are not geared to specific needs but based on two categories of basic and severe disability. A system of transitional payments, which slows down the effect of these changes on current claimants, is in operation.

Under the single payments system, grants, involving certain rights to payment backed up by a right to appeal to an independent tribunal, disbursed some £350 million in 1986/7. The Social Fund, limited in expenditure to £203 million, makes discretionary loans, and there is no right to appeal against decisions. The system involves an obligation to provide evidence of having sought help from charities, friends and relations, and even if this can be provided and the request deemed a reasonable one, no payment will be forthcoming if it involves the breach of cash limits.

Hardship is clearly caused to disabled people (40,000 on Government estimates, up to half a million according to the Disablement Income Group) who have been able to live in the community thanks to ARPs, which they will no longer receive. Some of these will doubtless be forced back into residential care as the value of the fixed transitional payment is eroded by rising costs and inflation, or as their condition leads to further special requirements.

For individuals hoping to make the move from institutional care to living in the community, the situation will be far more problematic than it was before. With no right to payment for essential items, and community care grants cash – limited and discretionary, both the initial move and its long-term viability are thrown into question.

Whilst other sections of the population are clearly severely effected by what the Bishop of Durham has referred to as the 'wickedness' of Government policies, disabled people experience these particular 'reforms' as an attack on their human rights, in so far as it renders it difficult, and in some cases impossible, to live outside institutions. The abolition of need-based ARPs, and the consequent treatment of disabled people as 'normal' welfare recipients, is by no means a desirable kind of 'normality'.

The field of housing provision is another area where the special needs of disabled people make it necessary to develop specialised knowledge and policies, and to recognise that disabled people are not 'normal'.

The vast majority of owner-occupied housing in Britain is unsuitable for people with major physical disabilities. The least satisfactory housing tends also to be that inhabited by sections of the population of which disabled people form a disproportionately large percentage – elderly people and people on low incomes.

Local authorities have always been the main providers of wheelchair and mobility adapted housing, and although the actual number of such dwellings has decreased between the periods 1970–81 and 1982–86 due to an overall decline in their house-building programme, the percentage of wheelchair and mobility adapted housing has increased in this period. As far as the main alternative source, housing associations, are concerned, an expansion in their activity in the 1980s has been accompanied by a declining proportion of adapted housing, and a decline in actual numbers (see Table). On current performance then, any contraction in local authority building programmes disproportionately disadvantages disabled people.

Table 1 Provision of wheelchair and mobility housing as % of total completions

	1970–81	1982–6
Local Authority		
Wheelchair	0.5	1.3
Mobility	2.6	6.8
Housing Association		
Wheelchair	0.7	0.4
Mobility	4.0	1.2

Table 2 Average number built per year

	1970–81	1982–6
Local Authority		
Wheelchair	483.3	281.4
Mobility	2364.3	1693.4
Housing Association		
Wheelchair	105.4	42.2
Mobility	587.2	138.0

Source: DOE housing construction statistics, cited in Morris, J. (1988)

The area of non-institutional housing which the Government intends to expand is the 'independent rented sector'. Whilst housing associations, whose performance as far as disabled people are concerned has been scrutinised above, are supposed to form an important element in this sector, the other component is private landlords.

Renting out property is intended to be made a more attractive proposition by a decontrolling of rents, the more general provision of shorthold tenancies, etc. None of these measures provides any incentive to carry out the adaptions necessary to make accommodation suitable for disabled people. Thus the decline in local authority housing budgets has a specific and disproportionately disadvantaging effect upon disabled people, which can only be obscurred if social workers, social analysts or disabled people themselves refer to us as 'normal'.

Again, Fry's recent study of difficulties confronted by disabled people in voting in the 1987 General Election (Fry, 1987) indicates a series of problems in the exercise of democratic rights which are to a large degree *sui generis*, and can only be understood through specific knowledge of disability.

Finally, as regards the Poll Tax, it is on the grounds that disabled people should be treated as 'normal' citizens that the Government has rejected the Allen amendment in the House of Lords, which would offer extra rebates to poor disabled people to cover the full cost of poll tax payments wherever they may live. This could force some disabled people out of their homes and into residential care. Brian Lamb, for the Spastics Society, pointed out (*Sunday Times* 17 July 1988) that disabled people often live in inner city areas which are likely to have high levels of community charge: 'A total rebate would cost the government peanuts, but the alternative may cost some disabled people their independence'.

Such concrete explorations of the effects of social policies and practices on disabled people indicates that any adequate understanding of the oppression of disabled people requires macro- and well as micro-level investigation. This is an area which can never be uncovered in simulation, and is only susceptible to research via detailed investigation. However these studies are conducted, it certainly cannot be in terms of the 'normality' of disabled people, since the concern must be to explicate the kinds and degrees of difference between the welfare needs of disabled people and the general population, with the multifarious features of 'normal' social life which prevent disabled people from being 'normal'.

As far as the training of social workers is concerned, I do not feel it is possible to deal with these issues adequately within a generic model of social work and a two year period of qualifying education.

The laudible prominence given in many courses to issues of anti-racism and anti-sexism being considered beyond the level of the superficial has the inevitable effect of contracting the time available for client groups whose oppression is less generally recognised. But at root the problem is not the amount of time devoted to issues of disability, so much as the way in which these issues are dealt with.

Given this, advances can still be made. One urgent task is to reverse the failure of the caring professions to recruit and train significant numbers of disabled people, which has happened partially through inertia and lack of pressure, but also because 'Social services traditionally looks after people with disabilities. To have to work alongside them is different from looking after them and requires a big shift in attitude' (Gledhill quoted in Caudry, 1987).

Whilst the presence of significant numbers of disabled social workers is not a sufficient condition for the development of social work practice which is appropriate to the real needs of disabled people, I certainly believe it is a necessary one. Social Services and educational institutions must be pressured to provide more posts and courses suitable for disabled people, for the advantage to us is a twofold one. Firstly it increases our career prospects, and, as such, is to be welcomed, but in addition to this it provides for the possibility of disabled welfare recipients dealing with someone who might possibly know what they're talking about.

Here issues of access, both to work situations and educational establishments, come to the fore. It must be recognised that this can involve issues beyond ramping and toilet doors. In my own institution, which operates on a number of sites, the relocation of social work teaching to a site suitable for disabled students has met resistance from those, both staff and students, who find the move an individual inconvenience, and are not prepared to take the issue of disability seriously if it means putting themselves out. But other problems involve the real disadvantaging of other disadvantaged groups, in particular women with young and school-age children, which might follow from the move. And these latter issues must be taken seriously, real conflicts of interest between disadvantaged groups recognised, and modes of handling them worked out, if opening the door to one group is not to involve slamming it in the face of another.

Alongside this, it is necessary for academics involved in social work education to take Disability seriously. To do this, of course, requires not only a will to do so, but the development of a body of theoretically based research upon which such teaching can be founded.

References

Abberley, P. (1987) 'The Concept of Oppression and the Development of a Social Theory of Disability' *Disability, Handicap and Society*, 2, 1, p. 5–19.

Beardshaw, V. (1988) *Last on the List: Community Services for People with Physical Disabilities*, London, Kings Fund Institute.

Brittan, A. and Maynard, M. (1984) *Sexism, Racism and Oppression*, Oxford, Basil Blackwell.

Carmen, E. *et al* (1981) 'Inequality and Women's Mental Health: An Overview' *American Journal of Psychiatry* 138, pp. 1319–30.

Caudry, A. (1987) 'Lambeth As Utopia' *New Society*, 31 July, pp. 8–10.

Challis, D. and Ferlie, E. (1988) The Myth of Generic Practice: Specialisation in Social Work, *Social Policy* 17, 1, p. 1–22.

Davis, F. (1961) 'Deviance and Disavowal' *Social Problems*, 9.

Foucault, M. (1967) *Madness and Civilisation*, London, Tavistock.

Fry, E. (1987) *Disabled People and the 1987 General Election*, London, Spastics Society.

Goffman, E. (1963) *Stigma – The Management of Spoilt Identity*, New Jersey, Prentice-Hall.

Gloag, D. (1984) 'Unmet Need in Chronic Disability', *British Medical Journal*, 289, pp. 211–2.

Hirst, M. (1985) 'Social Security and Insecurity: Young People with Disabilities in the U.K.' *Social Security Review*, 3, pp. 258–272.

Hunt, P. (1966) 'A critical condition in Hunt, P. (Ed) *Stigma*, London, Chapman, pp. 145–159.

Kammerer, R. C. (1940) 'An Exploratory Psychological Study of Crippled Children' *Psychological Record*, 4, Bloomington, Indiana, p. 47.

Katz, M. *et al* (1979) 'Reactions to Disability', *Journal of Personality*, 46, 3, p. 506.

Morris, J. (1988) *Freedom to Lose: Housing Policy and People with Disabilities*, London, Shelter.

Murphy, R. F. (1987) *The Body Silent*, New York, Henry Holt.

National Association of Citizens Advice Bureaux, Yorkshire and Humberside Area-Social Policy Group (1988) *Losers and Gainers – A Comparison of Benefits*, Leeds, CAB.

Oliver, M. (1983) *Social Work with Disabled People* Basingstoke, Macmillan.

Owen, M. J. (1985) 'A View of Disability in Current Social Work Literature' *American Behavioural Scientist*, 28, 3, pp. 397–417.

Owens, P. (1987) *Community Care and Severe Physical Disability*, London, Bedford Square Press.

Royal College of Physicians (1986) *The Young Disabled Adult* London, Royal College of Physicians.

Sacks, O. (1984) *A Leg to Stand On*, London, Duckworth.

Satyamurti, C. (1981) *Occupational Survival*, Oxford, Basil Blackwell.

Scull, A. (1979) *Museums of Madness: The Social Organisation of Insanity in Nineteenth Century England*, Harmondsworth, Allen Lane.

Scull, A. (1984) *Decarceration – Community Treatment and the Deviant*, Cambridge, Polity Press.

Seerbohm (1968) *Report of the Committee on Local Authority and Allied Personal Social Services* Cmnd 3703, London, HMSO.

Shearer, A. (1986) 'Wholeness and Handicap' *Holistic Medicine*, 1, pp. 105–113.

Sunday Times (1988) 17 July, p. A9.

Sutherland, A. (1981) *Disabled We Stand*, London, Souvenir Press.

Thomas, A. *et al* (1985) 'The Health and Social Needs of Physically Handicapped Young Adults: Are they being met by the Statutory Services?' *Developmental Medicine and Child Neurology* 27, 4, Supplement 50.

Turner, J. and Kepley, A. (1988) *Shake Up! – A Guide to the New Social Security Benefits*, London, BBC Office Printing.

Chapter Five

'I'm Not Handicapped – I'm Different': 'Normalisation', Hospital-Care, and Mental Handicap

Mano Candappa and Robert G. Burgess

Introduction

Some researchers have suggested that the problem of mental handicap is not the result of one handicap, but a combination of factors. Firstly, the individual's own mental handicap; secondly, an imposed or acquired handicap (through deficiencies in the conditions of life created for him/her by society, or through the attitudes of people s/he has contact with) which adds to the primary handicap; and thirdly, the awareness of being mentally handicapped – which could lead to '..distorted self-concepts, defence mechanisms, closing in on inner problems and defeatist allowances. . . .' (Nirje, 1970, 64). This chapter (in common with our study) investigates this assertion, focusing primarily on how life conditions, and the perceptions or attitudes of carers influence the self-image of people with a mental handicap and the image they present to the outside world.

The Research

The research project on which our study is based, was commissioned by the West Midlands Regional Health Authority. The study was designed by Burgess, and involved the use of qualitative methods of social investigation to study the skill requirements of staff involved in community care. Burgess had used this approach in educational settings (Burgess, 1984) and argued that techniques such as observation, participant observation, unstructured interviews and the use of documentary evidence would give access to perceptions held by those individuals who worked with mentally handicapped people.

Accordingly, the project proposal involved case studies of two hospitals that were used to house mentally handicapped people, followed by further in-depth investigations of work with mentally handicapped people in community settings. A research fellow (Mano Candappa) was appointed to the project with responsibility for the fieldwork. Candappa was attached to both hospitals where she joined a shift in order to share the life and work of the staff. At the start of the fieldwork, it was envisaged that she would be 'an extra pair of hands' available to staff, but occasions arose when she was asked to assume responsibilities of a full-time member of staff (despite the fact that she has no qualifications or training in nursing). Much of the material in this paper is therefore taken from Candappa's fieldnotes that were collected through extensive participant observation.

This research forms part of a broader range of issues concerned with community care, staff perceptions, and skills assessment which it was possible to examine at the hospitals we studied. In both cases access was provided to staff, to wards and to formal and informal gatherings. The study developed using a combination of participant observation and unstructured interviews (Burgess, 1982, 1984) to focus on staff perceptions of their work that were examined in relation to documentary materials on policy issues. On the basis of these data a series of connecting cases are established to highlight some fundamental social processes associated with work among mentally handicapped people in the hospital we call Manor Hall. In analysing our data we have taken the normalisation principle as our point of reference. We thus ask: what do our own data tell us about relationships between staff and residents and about normalisation in practice at Manor Hall Hospital? Firstly, however, because the term 'normalisation' is open to interpretation, it is relevant, for the purpose of clarity, to discuss the principle of normalisation.

The Principle of Normalisation

The principle of normalisation has been widely discussed (see Nitsch *et al*, 1980, Rose-Ackerman, 1982) and has been the subject of much confusion and misunderstanding. As Wolfensberger (1980a) suggests, these confusions may have arisen because the term is derived from the word 'normal' which had an established meaning, but which could be misleading in terms of the normalisation principle. Wolfensberger defines normalisation as:

use of culturally normative means to offer [devalued] persons life conditions at least as good as that of average citizens, and to as much as possible enhance or support their behaviour, appearances, experiences, status and reputation . . .

(Wolfensberger, 1980b, 8)

Wolfensberger's definition stems from his perception that a person becomes devalued not through 'differentness' itself but through *negatively valued 'differentness'*, which is socially, subjectively, and variably defined, varying from culture to culture, and time to time (Wolfensberger 1980b). As such, he suggests that this devaluation ' . . . can be reduced or eliminated either by (a) changing the perceptions or values of the perceiver, or (b) minimizing the differentness or stigma of deviancy that activates the perceiver's devaluation . . .' (Wolfensberger, 1980b, 13). Normalisation seeks to address the first of the two options indirectly via the second.

Wolfensberger further suggests that seeking to minimise 'differentness' or stigma through normalisation has several implications which may not be obvious. These include:

(a) Enhancing the cultural stereotype of a deviant group is often more important than sizeable short-term or local clinical benefits.

(b) Elimination of negative deviancy image juxtaposition, and enhancing the 'representation' of persons is often as important as normalising their behaviour.

(c) Use of 'conservative' (more valued) alternatives from a range of normative options.

(d) Avoidance of deviant person juxtapositions.

(e) Age separation, and age-appropriate structures.

(f) Dispersal instead of congregation of deviant persons.

(g) Physical placement of services into culture-typical contexts.

(h) Dignity of risk.

(i) De-emphasis of staff-client distinctions.

(j) Separation of the domiciliary function. (Wolfensberger, 1980b, 19)

Wolfensberger's definition of normalisation and its implications have been used as a guide in this study – since it is in his work that the principle is given its broadest interpretation, and its process is specified in greatest detail (cf. Bank-Mikkelsen, 1980; Nirje, 1970; Wolfensberger, 1980a and b).

While the principle of normalisation is part of the language of the present philosophy of care for mentally handicapped people in Britain, the question we ask is whether, and to what extent, the normalisation principle is accepted, or indeed understood, by carers in one of the mental handicap hospitals we studied.

'Normalisation' in Practice

A commitment to the principle of normalisation was expressed in policy documents for mental handicap services in the District Health Authority where our study took place. But, as often happens, a gap between rhetoric and reality was observed over a four month period of fieldwork at one mental handicap hospital. This is not to say, however, that the Health Authority would claim that the principle of normalisation is put into practice in its hospitals: on the contrary, the Authority acknowledges this shortcoming.

Moreover, a hospital situation for mentally handicapped people is admittedly against the principle of normalisation itself, for these hospitals correspond to Goffman's characterisation of the 'total institution': '. . . places of residence and work where a large number of like-situated individuals . . . together lead an enclosed, formally-administered round of life . . .' (Goffman, 1962, p. xiii) with restricted contact with the outside world. Yet even a hospital context is open to aspects of normalisation, such as de-emphasis of staff-client distinctions, the dignity of risk, and so on. Indeed, it has been argued that the hospital should be used as a normalising 'training environment' (see Gunzburg, 1970). But within the process of change, remnants of old beliefs and practices do persist; and it is these tensions that our study seeks to demonstrate.

Manor Hall is small by mental handicap hospital standards, having had 125 adult residents at the time of the study in 1987/88. All residents had their own clothing; they were encouraged to have their own personal belongings; and had their own 'space' on the wards. So outwardly, residents appeared reasonably well-cared for. But how far the normalisation principle could be put into practice within the constraints of a hospital situation depends to a great extent on how staff perceive their client group and interact with them. Our study therefore focuses on Manor Hall staff – their perceptions and the roles they play in relation to the residents, and how these could affect public perceptions of mentally handicapped people and the residents' own self-image.

Staff perceptions and staff client roles

The assumption behind the normalisation principle is that the people putting it into practice perceive the client group as valued. But some staff in the hospital behaved in a manner that would give the lie to such an assumption. For example, Candappa observed:

> They [Joyce and Bridget] never use the teaspoons from the ward, but they've got their own hidden away . . . They deign to use the bread supplied by the hospital, but they have to have a fresh loaf which they keep separate from those the residents touch and use – it has to be an unopened loaf before they take anything for themselves out of it. The same goes for the Flora [margarine]: it has to be an unopened packet. And as for the milk, if the bottle has even a little bit taken out of it, they wouldn't touch it but would take an unopened bottle. So today, seeing me making myself a cup of coffee . . . Bridget handed me a partly used bottle of milk, saying, 'Use this, I only opened it just now' – as though I'd catch something dreadful if I used one of the others . . .

Contrary to seeing the hospital residents as valued, it would seem that there was a strong sense of 'them' and 'us' among some staff at Manor Hall. Indeed, in a ward for low dependency residents that hardly ever involved messy work, Bridget always wore a plastic apron over her own clothes while on duty, which suggests that such 'rituals' are more to do with institutional patterns of behaviour (where maintaining a social distance between groups is the norm) than with questions of hygiene.

Moreover, there were occasions when it seemed that staff did not perceive the residents as being wholly human. For example, on one afternoon when a concert had been arranged at the hospital, Candappa recorded in her fieldnotes:

> We were all seated in anticipation of the performers' arrival. . . . Then Edith [a woman who could not speak, but seems in full possession of her other faculties] . . . came in through the main doors. Immediately a cry went up from Pauline [a nurse], Ruth [a nursing auxiliary (NA)] and ward staff who had come along with residents who are wheelchair-bound and who were at the back of the hall. The cry we all could hear was 'Ah, ah, ah, ah,' – mocking the sound Edith makes when she tries to draw someone's attention. . . . Edith looked at them, and made no response at all but just went and sat down. . . .
>
> [A little while later] Pauline got up and went to the main doors.

When she was walking back to her seat again, Katie [a resident] got up from where she was seated beside Dennis [a nurse] and started to walk down the hall. While she walked she put her hand between her legs and kept scratching herself. Dennis looked at her over his glasses and said, 'We don't do that sort of thing in polite circles Katie!' Katie said, 'What?' And Dennis said again, 'I said, "We don't do that sort of thing in polite circles" '. Katie continued scratching just the same. Pauline walked behind her, exaggeratedly mimicking her action, to the huge enjoyment of the assembled staff. . . .

A few days later a similar incident took place, when a group of residents and staff were preparing to leave the hospital by minibus for a local sports centre. Candappa wrote:

We were one short – Joan [a resident] . . . had still not arrived. But Pauline thought it was time for us to leave, so we all got seated . . . [Then] Pauline was saying to Mike [the driver] 'Let's go', and we were off. As we turned into the main driveway we could see Joan walking towards us. Seeing her Pauline said, 'Quick, put your foot on the gas!' Laughingly Mike obliged; and we sped off leaving Joan behind. Still looking at Joan, Pauline went 'Bawhhh!' – imitating the way Joan often bawls out. . . .

These incidents seem to suggest that if residents were perceived as being human, some staff did not recognise that they had feelings or senses. And as such, residents could serve as objects of fun for some staff. Moreover, such staff behaviour could be described as unprofessional conduct.

There were other examples, moreover, that demonstrate the way in which staff perceive the residents, and the whole staff-resident relationship. It seems to us that some staff see themselves in a custodial role, which presupposes that because residents are mentally handicapped they are incapable of performing functions, or making decisions, which staff perform on their behalf. For example, Candappa recorded in her fieldnotes that one day

After lunch Bridget suggested that we clean out and tidy the residents lockers [and] I went along with her . . . I asked her if the residents wouldn't mind her coming and clearing their lockers out while they were not in. The idea didn't seem to have even struck her. She looked at me strangely and said 'Oh no!'

One of the lockers we cleared out was Robert's. She said 'Robert never tidies up'; and so we took out his shirts and jumpers and folded them, and his trousers and hung them up. . . . Then we went to his drawers. When she opened the first one Bridget said to me, 'Just look at this, I'm sure you've never seen so many dirty pictures'. I looked in the drawer and saw about five to six pages from a woman's magazine: they were all pictures advertising underwear. They certainly weren't 'girly' magazine stuff nor could they be considered porn in any sense of the word. Bridget took every single one of them out of the drawer, crumpled them up and put them in the waste bin. She said, 'You wouldn't believe that one man could have so many dirty pictures'. Then she looked at me and said 'You know what he does? He looks at these and masturbates' – with a look of disgust. (By now she had destroyed all the pictures). I said to her 'Oh! but isn't that fairly common? I thought many normal people do that'. She gave me a very strange look but said nothing. Then she found another picture. This one she approved of and she said, 'Ah this is a nice picture, let's put that out shall we?' and she put it out. I glanced at it, and saw what looked like a picture of the Queen when she was about seven years old standing beside her corgis. . . .

In this instance Bridget's behaviour suggests that, as custodian, she considers it her right (or perhaps even duty) to go through residents' belongings without their permission and dispose of whatever she considers to be unnecessary. Secondly, she seems to consider herself guardian of Robert's (or any other resident's) morals, so she could destroy the pictures she considered to be distasteful.

The question of how much choice staff allow residents is also illustrated in the following set of events, again involving the resident Robert.

Robert attends a local Social Education Centre (SEC) three days a week, and on two of the three days he used to catch the bus on time and attended regularly. But on the third day, a Friday, he always missed his bus and stayed on at the hospital. When questioned he would say that the bus left without him. Staff then ensured that he left the ward well in time and stood watching until he reached the pickup point. But he still missed his bus. Then the nurse on duty rang up the SEC to find out the bus driver's story. She was told that if Robert was at the pickup point on time, he would make an excuse saying he was going for cigarettes or some such thing, and never came back. Robert was a chain smoker, so as a deterrent his cigarettes were reduced – to no avail. And no-one seemed to have an explanation for Robert's behaviour. Then came another Friday, the day of the concert:

. . . the art therapy session was to continue for those who preferred art therapy to the concert . . . Robert [was one of those who] opted to stay on. Lucy [the art therapist], Pauline, Peter [who was in charge of the therapies], Ruth and I stood talking together. The conversation turned to why Robert doesn't go to the SEC on a Friday. Hearing our conversation he said, 'Why can't I go Monday, Tuesday and Wednesday?' Lucy pounced on that. She said, 'Yes, Robert really enjoys painting, look at this' and held up a picture with trees and animals. Robert had done that. She continued, 'Look, he really loves painting, I think it's cruel to deprive him of it. Why can't they arrange with the SEC for the days *he'd* like to go, so that he could stay here on a Friday?' Peter joined in: 'Yes, of course they don't think of things like that when they arrange placements do they?'

Here we find arrangements being made for a resident without reference to his wishes. It also demonstrates the custodial role staff see for themselves in relation to residents by taking decisions on their behalf and making choices for them. In this case, however, we find the resident concerned attempting to circumvent arrangements made by staff. But it is interesting that he gave his reasons for missing SEC only to the art therapist (who is an outsider to the hospital), and not to the ward staff.

These field observations suggest that many staff perceive the residents as devalued and different from themselves, in some cases by calling the residents' humanity into question. By definition staff see themselves as custodians, making arrangements and decisions on behalf of residents assuming that they are incapable of making these for themselves. This perception of residents by staff is not necessarily confined to the hospital, but projects itself onto the outside world, so that onlookers can perceive the difference and social distance between staff and residents, as the following case study of a 'trip' to Blackpool demonstrates.

Staff–client roles and outsiders perceptions

A half-day trip to see the Blackpool illuminations had been arranged by Mr Sherif, the Charge Nurse of the ward Candappa was working on. A coach had been hired for the trip: the party consisted of twenty-six residents and six staff from the ward, and, in addition, five residents (of whom four were in wheel chairs) and four staff from another ward – making a total of forty-one in all. Residents dressed in their best clothes for the occasion and staff too wore smart clothes. Before leaving the hospital, drugs for all concerned were measured out into little containers and packed into a small box. Mr Sherif had charged all staff with the duty of seeing that the drugs chart and drugs box were not left behind. The coach arrived around 2 pm and the party set off soon after. Candappa recorded in her fieldnotes:

> . . . I picked up the drugs box and the drugs schedule, which seemed to have been forgotten, and went along with everybody else. . . .
>
> . . . When I was getting onto the coach carrying this drugs box and drugs chart, Joyce said to Dave [another staff member] 'We don't usually take this with us!' – pointing to the drugs chart. He shook his head looking at me, so I said that Mr Sherif had asked us to take it. They both shrugged . . . [and then we got in and found ourselves seats]. . . .
>
> [On the way we stopped at a motorway restaurant for pastries, tea and coffee] . . . When we got in Mr Sherif said 'Let us get all our people on one side.' So our residents were duly seated down. Then he went up to the counter and got a whole tray of Danish pastries and went round himself doling these out to everyone, including staff. I don't know why he did this; I thought it was fairly inappropriate behaviour in terms of normalisation. But Joyce seemed to be impressed, and she said to Bridget and me, 'He the best charge nurse we have at Manor Hall: he really love these people, and when he take them out he want to give them a real good time . . .' [Tea and coffee were served by restaurant staff. And then we were on our way again.]
>
> [Later in the evening we stopped at a pub in a village outside Blackpool for dinner.] . . . The first thing we had to do when we went in was to see that all the residents were toileted [as we had also done at the motorway stop before]. So we all trooped into the toilets and it was a while before we got everybody seated. . . . [And then] Mr Sherif called me and said, 'Bring that thing, the drugs.' So obediently I picked up the drugs box and the drugs list and went up to him. He was standing under the only bright light in the room; he'd got his glasses on, and he asked me to place this drugs box on the table beside him. Then he got out his pen and started ticking off the drugs though they had already been measured out and put into little containers before we left the hospital. I had to stand beside him while Marjorie (a nursing auxiliary) walked up and down handing out these drugs. Martin, a very capable resident, was called up and asked to go up to the bar and ask for a glass of water. Then his medicine was quite obviously mixed in with the water and given to him. . . .

When we'd sat down again I said to Marjorie, 'Is it always done like this?' She must have not noticed anything strange because she said, 'Oh yes, the drugs have always got to be given out'.

After the drugs had been given out, Mr Sherif went around asking all our residents what they would like to drink. Some of the staff were also doing the same at other tables. Mr Sherif then gave the total order for our group (while the other Charge Nurse looked after his group). Again Mr Sherif went around himself handing out these drinks. . . . Then he gave the orders for the dinner, and again it was he who went up to the counter and carried the plates to our residents and staff. . . .

The residents and staff from our ward sat separately from those from the other ward probably because of the problem of mixing up monies. But the staff from our ward sat separately from the residents. (It wasn't quite like that with the other ward, perhaps because some residents had to be helped with eating). And then Martin called out to us from the other end of the room, 'Why are you all sitting there together?'. . . .

The meal over, we piled into the coach and drove on to Blackpool. Once there we drove slowly along the seafront so we could all see the lights. Then we started back for Manor Hall. We must have been in Blackpool for just half an hour. As the coach turned out of town, Marjorie exclaimed, 'Oh! was that it then?' I too felt it was a bit of an anticlimax . . .

[On the way back, around 10.00pm, we stopped off at another motorway restaurant. There] . . . as before we first got the residents toileted and seated. Then Mr Sherif called Marjorie, Joyce and me up to the counter and asked us to carry plates of buns, tea cakes, pastries and whatever was around and serve these to our residents. Next he asked us to carry trays of coffee and tea around to the tables as well. All this we did – while restaurant staff and other customers watched. . . .

[That was our last stop. And it was midnight before we got back to the hospital again].

This 'trip' has implications in terms of the normalisation principle. Firstly, even though it may be argued that a coachload of sightseers is in keeping with social norms, congregating a group of thirty-one mentally handicapped people, of whom four are in wheelchairs, does nothing to enhance the group's image, and in fact drew attention to aspects of their appearance and/or manners that people tend to devalue. The whole party trooping into motorway restaurants and into a public house could therefore have had this effect. In the same way, staff attending to the groups toileting, especially at the pub, drew attention to the fact that many of the party needed help. So too, having seating arranged by staff, and food and drink orders collected and served by staff at the pub and restaurants would not have enhanced the cultural stereotype of mentally handicapped people, but could in fact have served to reinforce the stereotype. Indeed, it suggests a social division between those people who are mentally handicapped and the rest of the population.

Secondly, throughout the trip the staff-client distinction was emphasised rather than de-emphasised: staff were seen to be different from their client group. Staff sat separately from hospital residents, they carried their food and drink to them, and attended to their toileting. But this same behaviour also illustrates the tensions between normalization and a previously valued model of care. When the Charge Nurse walked around serving cakes and pastries to his group, the remark made by one of his staff suggests that she saw his behaviour as 'caring' and therefore valued. Indeed, there are strong parallels between such behaviour and the care of children. The tension between competing models of care will need to be addressed, then, for normalization to be practiced.

However, the very public display of administering drugs at the pub could have served no useful purpose. The drugs could easily, and more appropriately, have been administered on the coach either before or after the meal. Not only did this incident emphasise the staff-client distinction but it also demonstrated to onlookers that the client group was in need of regulated medication, and could therefore have reduced the group's image even further. But a remark made by a staff member at the time suggests that she did not perceive these implications.

Since many staff see their client group as different from themselves in a negative sense, this is the image they present to the world at large. But whether, and to what extent, such staff perceptions influence their clients' self-image is an important question especially in relation to normalization. It is to this topic that we now turn.

Staff–client roles and residents' self image

We begin by turning to a series of related case materials to examine some factors that could affect residents' self-perceptions. Our first example is on the theme of self-help and dignity. Candappa recorded in her fieldnotes:

[One morning when residents were getting dressed] . . . I found Dave, this time not shaving anyone [as was usually the case] but actually supervising residents shaving themselves. . . . He was working with Ed when I walked in. . . . [It took a lot of persuasion for Dave to get Ed to attempt to shave himself. He succeeded in the end, but Dave had to finish the job properly].

Dave next called Tom . . . [who] I think is quite sharp. When Dave said, 'Come on Tom, it's time for a shave', Tom came willingly. But when he said, 'Here's the brush, now would you like to soap your face?' Tom laughed and said, 'You do it'. Dave replied, 'Come on Tom, you can do it'. Tom countered, 'Me patient, you staff, you do it'. . . . [After some coaxing and a bribe of an extra cigarette, Tom was persuaded to shave himself – which he did very competently and with no help from Dave.]

In this instance we find a staff member trying to help two residents discover their own potential and in doing so taking the risk that either of them could injure themselves. But he meets with resistance at the beginning from both residents, who have to be coaxed into accepting the challenge. Both residents were subsequently found to be capable of shaving themselves. But Tom's comment seems to suggest that the staff-resident relationship (as illustrated above) has been such that staff perform a range of tasks, for and on behalf of residents. Residents are thus not encouraged to test their potential, which therefore remains undiscovered. Moreover, residents then accept a passive role which reinforces a social division between them and the staff.

But apart from the role they play in relation to staff, it is also interesting to examine other ways in which residents perceive themselves. This we do in the following two examples taken from Candappa's fieldnotes:

[One afternoon as I was walking away from the dining room having helped with serving the dinners] . . . Sue [a student nurse] came up behind me laughing, and said, 'Do you know what Jim said to Cathy?' [another student nurse]

'No, what did he say?' I said.

'He was doing something or other', she said, 'and Cathy, seeing that, called out "Jim, stop behaving like a stupid idiot". Jim replied, "I'm in here because I'm a stupid idiot" and he walked off beating his head' [which he often does when he is upset].

Here the resident perceives himself as 'a stupid idiot', but whether his self-perception was gained through staff or public attitudes or in some other way can only be speculated on. But the fact that some residents do perceive that staff view them negatively cannot be discounted. And that

Jim perceives some futility in his situation is indicated by the way he beat his head as he walked away.

However, not every resident sees him/herself as 'a stupid idiot' – as another set of Candappa's observations suggest:

> [One morning when I was working in the therapy department Tom walked in, and seeing me, came up for a chat. I asked him how he was, and we talked for a bit] . . . Meanwhile Cathy and Ruth were also having a conversation, which I wasn't giving ear to, but I heard the word 'handicapped' come from one of them. I think that somehow Tom must have been listening with one ear to what they were saying because he then said, 'I'm not handicapped, I'm different'. I was caught off guard and said, 'What did he say?' The room seemed to have suddenly become quieter; Cathy and Ruth were looking at Tom. Then Cathy said, 'He said, "I'm not handicapped, I'm different" '.

Here Tom, unlike Jim, has a positive self-image, which indicates that sometimes, at least, positive attitudes he perceives outweigh the negative. Again, where and from whom he receives these perceptions can only be speculation at this stage and is an area for further research.

Conclusion

People with a mental handicap have been viewed with contempt and derision in this country from early times down to this century (see Ryan and Thomas, 1980). For example, Tredgold, writing in 1908, had described 'idiots' (a description then used for one category of people with mental handicap) as having '. . . no intelligence, and no consciousness of pleasure and pain; in fact their mental state is one entire negation . . .' (Tredgold 1908, 171). Indeed, even as recently as 1961, Stafford-Clark, a psychiatrist, has claimed that 'idiots' '. . . are in fact considerably less intelligent than domestic animals . . .' (Stafford Clarke, 1961, 89). Our study suggests that perceptions such as those of Tredgold and Stafford-Clarke are still alive among carers of mentally handicapped people today, even though the current philosophy of care in Britain is based on the recognition of a mentally handicapped person's human dignity.

In our introduction we have quoted Nirje as saying that the problem of mental handicap is the result of a combination of three factors, one of which is the attitudes of people he has contact with. Further on, we have referred to Wolfensberger's analysis that a person becomes devalued through negatively valued differentness, and attempted to show how normalisation seeks to address this problem. In our study, however, we have found that a basic assumption behind the normalisation principle, i.e. that those practising it see their client group as valued, is notably absent among many staff at Manor Hall. Moreover, in some instances we find disturbing echoes of a previous era, such as when inmates of London's Bethlem Asylum were mocked for public entertainment (see Skultans, 1979).

However, this is not to say that we disparage a devalued and low-paid workforce, a high proportion of whom are professionally unqualified, both nationally and at Manor Hall itself. We are also aware that a hospital situation, by definition, does create a relationship of dependency between carers and those they care for. Moreover, while we have drawn attention to the emphasis on the staff-client distinction, we concede that this could be part of the process of socialisation into an institutional regime. The problem seems to be that many staff do not critically assess their own role.

We have demonstrated that tensions exist between the new and the old: between normalisation and the previously-valued model of care. While pointing to the parallel between child-care and custodial care, we would like to suggest that custodial care could also be paternalistic, so that love and dominance become interchangeable. Furthermore, interviews conducted subsequent to the period of participant observation revealed that while staff were aware of the term 'normalisation', many of them were unaware of its implications. This may explain some of the tensions between competing models of care.

Our own study, which adds to the existing documentation on oppression of people with a mental handicap (see for example DHSS, 1969; Ryan and Thomas, 1980), strongly suggests that addressing the values and perceptions of carers is one of the primary tasks of normalisation. But if mentally handicapped people are to be released from oppression, perhaps society should look beyond normalisation and seek to rationalise its attitudes towards devalued people.

Acknowledgements

We are indebted to the Health Authority (that must remain anonymous) for sponsoring this study. In addition, we would like to thank John Bishop, Caroline Currer, Sylvia Lindoe, Margaret Stacey, and participants at the 'Disability, Handicap and Policy Conference' for their helpful comments on this paper. Finally, we would like to thank our project secretary

Carole Cox for her support in transcribing field materials and typing and retyping this paper with great skill.

References

Bank-Mikkelsen, N. E. (1980) 'Denmark' in Flynn R. J., and Nitsch, K. E. (Eds) *Normalization, Social Integration and Community Services*, Baltimore, University Park Press, pp. 51–70.

Burgess, R. G. (1982) (Ed) *Field Research: A Sourcebook and Field Manual*, London, Allen and Unwin.

Burgess, R. G. (1984) *In the Field: An Introduction to Field Research*, London, Allen and Unwin

DHSS (1969) *Report of the Committee of Enquiry into Allegations of Ill-Treatment of Patients and other Irregularities at the Ely Hospital, Cardiff*, The Howe Report, London, HMSO (Cmnd. 3975)

Goffman, E. (1962) *Asylums*, Chicago, Aldine.

Gunzburg, H. C. (1970) 'The hospital as a normalizing training environment', *Journal of Mental Subnormality* 16, 2, pp. 71–83.

Nitsch, K. E., Armour, A. and Flynn, R. J. (1980) 'A normalization bibliography' in Flynn, R. J. and Nitsch, K. E. (Eds) *Normalization, Social Integration and Community Services* Baltimore, University, Park Press, pp. 395–409.

Nirje, B. (1970) 'The normalization principle – implications and comments', *Journal of Mental Subnormality*, 16, 2, pp. 62–70.

Rose-Ackerman, S. (1982) 'Mental retardation and society: the ethics and politics of normalization' *Ethics*, 39, October, pp. 81–101.

Ryan, J. and Thomas F. (1980) *The Politics of Mental Handicap*, Harmondsworth, Penguin.

Skultans, V. (1979) *English Madness* London, Routledge and Kegan Paul.

Stafford-Clark, D. (1961) *Psychiatry Today*, Harmondsworth, Penguin.

Tredgold, A. (1908) *Mental Deficiency (Amentia)*, London, Baillere Tindall.

Wolfensberger, W. (1980a) 'The definition of normalization' in Flynn, R. J. and Nitsch, K. E. (Eds) *Normalization, Social Integration and Community Services*, Baltimore, University Park Press, pp. 71–115.

Wolfensberger, W (1980b) 'A brief overview of the principle of normalization' in Flynn, R. J., and Nitsch, K. E. (Eds) *op. cit.*, pp. 7–30.

Chapter Six

The 6/75 Family Assessment and Evaluation Program

Marion Blythman & Frieda Spivack

Introduction

This chapter deals with the assessment and evaluation of multi-risk families in an urban setting, in Brooklyn, New York City.

Since 1987 the US Federal Government, through its legislation PL 99.457, requires that States will provide a free appropriate public education to all handicapped children aged three through five, by the fiscal year 1990.

The purpose of the 6/75 Program is to develop and implement a cohesive plan to meet the special needs of multi-risk families i.e. the 6 per cent of families reported as utilizing 75 per cent of all public, mental health and social services in the USA. Such families represent all, or a combination of, disabling factors such as poverty, homelessness, isolation, teenage single parenthood, substance abuse, poor general health and recurring life threatening crises.

Procedures are aimed to cultivate partnership and provide for the maximum degree of parental participation and empowerment. There is a clear definition of the needs of the families and the roles and responsibilities of all concerned. A system of communication has been established, which is aimed to ensure an effective and speedy flow of information to all team members, particularly parents.

The claim of the 6/75 Program is that even one trusted and effective agency, assessing, counselling and educating, and delivering health and other therapeutic services, can both improve the quality of life of these multi-risk families and reduce the 6/75 ratio, through:

(a) rehabilitating families incapacitated on account of poverty, social problems and handicapping conditions;
(b) helping families become more self-sufficient;

(c) improving their feelings of autonomy and self-worth;

and by so doing reduce the present high financial cost to the providing agencies by millions of dollars.

As can be seen from Figure 1, this is a claim that has been acknowledged by the US Federal Government. Clearly, welfare, health-care, medical and social services combined can run away with billions of dollars. For example, in a book *Within Our Reach* which details the benefits of educational and other interventions, Lisbeth Schorr reports that eight babies from South Dakota whose mothers had no pre-natal care needed neonatal intensive care which cost in total half a million dollars. Yet, as illustrates Figure 1, the provision of adequate pre-school education alone can save billions of dollars in later social costs.

Figure 1

Cost-Effective Programs

WIC: FOOD FOR WOMEN, INFANTS, CHILDREN

Reduces infant mortality and increases birthweight. Only 44 percent of these eligible participate.

$1 Investment in prenatal component can save $3 in short-term hospital costs.

PRENATAL CARE

Reduces low birthweight, prematurity and infant mortality.

$1 Investment can save $3.38 in cost of care for low-birthweight infants.

MEDICAID

Decreases neonatal and infant mortality, and abnormalities through Early Periodic Screening Services.

$1 spent on comprehensive prenatal care for Medicaid recipients save $2 in infant's first-year care.

CHILDHOOD IMMUNISATION

Reduces vaccine-preventable childhood diseases like rubella, mumps, measles and polio.

$1 spent on Childhood Immunisation Program saves $10 in later medical costs.

PRESCHOOL EDUCATION

Increases school success, employ-ability and self-esteem. Less than 20 percent of those eligible are participating in Head Start.

$1 spent on preschool education can save $6 in later social costs.

Source: USA House of Representatives Select Committee on Children, Youth & Families, 1987.

Background

Before one can begin to describe and analyze the education of pre-school handicapped children in the City of New York, there are some points which should be understood about the USA generally and its educational system in particular.

From outside of America it is difficult to appreciate in real terms what a wealthy country the USA actually is. Not only is the standard of living of the majority of Americans measurably higher than in any other society, but the level of expectation is equally high in terms of education, leisure and day-to-day living. The educational system is particularly impressive in terms of accommodation, facilities, personnel, teaching aids and equipment. It is open and accountable. Traditionally, both privately and publicly, there is general and genuine concern about the standard of education and how effectively it is delivered to the children of this 'nation of nations'.

Unfortunately for some, as in most Western countries, this enormous wealth is not evenly divided. This is a society which is divided into two kinds of families, a dual system with 'roughly half our children somewhat randomly, but inexorably, born without a fair chance', as the well-known New York Democratic Senator Daniel Moynihan writes in the *New York Times*, 25 September 1988. 'In a society', he continues, 'with more than enough to go around, poverty is a form of bad luck. Children have the most of it'. Sadly, the USA, with all of its resources, is the first nation in history where not only are the children the poorest group of the population, but this problem is increasing and intensifying from year to year.

The USA is a prime example of a country where the rich are all the time getting richer, and the poor poorer, with the top 10 per cent of the population owning 65 per cent of all the net worth of the nation, and the bottom 50 per cent worth only 4 per cent. Forty-five per cent of the children in the schools of wealthy New York are on welfare and live well below the poverty line i.e. with an annual income of less than $9500 for a family of four.

This population occupies 'decaying buildings in crowded neighbourhoods with a few opportunities for meaningful work outside the unstable low skill service sector'. Recent studies of poverty in the City indicate that conditions have become worse for some groups and that their future prospects are bleak (Tobier, 1984).

As reported in the *New York Times*, 3 September 1988, 'Tenants here are fearful, desperate, afraid to ride the elevators, afraid to answer their apartment doors, because they don't know who is knocking. At Smith

Houses, as at many of the other 316 projects that are home to 600,000 New Yorkers, mainly the poor and the elderly, the problem is crack, the cheap smokable cocaine derivative whose ravaging effects on whole neighbourhoods were officially recognised about two years ago'.

Recent figures show, in addition, that in New York City 20 per cent of child bearing mothers are teenagers (some homeless), and that one of every 61 babies born in New York City in December 1987 carried Aids antibodies (*New York Times*, 13 January 1988). This population i.e. the poor and teenage mothers (estimated at some 6 per cent of the total population) uses 75 per cent of the child welfare, social, hospital, substance abuse, high-risk infant care, housing and legal aid resources of the city.

The teenage mothers of the 6/75 group are generally unsupported and practically all on welfare. They have, in fact, responsibilities before they have had the chance to grow up or become bread-winners. Many are drug and substance abusers and come over as retarded and emotionally disturbed though much of this can be ascribed to the living conditions in which they find themselves, and the way in which they have accommodated to these. They are poor, unemployed, homeless, oppressed and depressed by the conditions of their lives. On the whole they lack any stable income or support and are particularly subject to life threatening crises arising from illness, crime, etc.

The children do not escape the consequences. As reported by the Ford Foundation, 'More than half of the twelve million children who live in families headed up by women, are living in poverty' (1985). At any given moment, about one child in four in the USA is born into poverty. More than one in three will be on welfare at some time or other during their lives, and around 50 per cent will live in a single parent family (generally female) with all that implies in terms of a serious reduction of income. In Brooklyn, for example, the infant mortality rate is over 30 per 1000 at or before birth, a figure worse than that of many third world countries.

Some children in New York City show deficiency diseases due to poor nutrition. Many babies deemed as 'failure to thrive' are living in accommodation which is vermin infested and filthy. Many of these children show distinct signs of emotional neglect to a pathological degree. As Dr Eleanor Stokes, Executive Director of the National Center for Clinical Infant Programs, points out in a hard hitting editorial in a new journal, *Infants and Young Children* (1988 Vol. 1) 'The statistics bear out the, nation's inattention to its children in the first years of life: 1%–2% of children are identified as having disabilities at the time of birth. In contrast 8%–9% are identified as having disabling conditions, and as many as 11%–12% are estimated to have significant developmental delays by the time they enter school'.

There is, therefore, a marked discontinuity for some people living in New York City in 1988 between the great American dream and the reality of their day to day living. As Sally Tomlinson points out in an article entitled 'Why Johnny Can't Read' (1987), where she applies the theories of the Frankfurt School to an analysis of what has happened to children with special educational needs: '. . . in noting the sharp contrasts between the optimistic, scientific, confident rhetoric of progress and egalitaniarism and the actual inequality of treatment of minorities and low socio–economic groups, and the handicapped and the less able, critical theorists were able to inject a note of scepticism into the often self-congratulatory Western view of the "progress" and humanity of technologically advanced post industrial societies.'

The Educational System

Nevertheless, there is universal public and private adherence to an egalitarian philosophy. This is quite fundamental to the American system of public education, aimed as it is to provide:

(a) a free and appropriate education for all (from kindergarten, through twelve years of public education);
(b) a system of public schools, open to all;
(c) for the most part, a common curriculum for all children regardless of background.

While it took till well on in the twentieth century for this egalitarianism to encompass the whole American population, particularly the poor and the blacks, it should be noted that when they were finally included, it was because, in fact (in terms of the constitution) they could not be denied their right to a free and appropriate education. The question, as with handicapped and disabled pupils, was not **what** this education was to be but **where** it was to be delivered. While the issues around the separation and segregation of the black population had to be bitterly fought out in the Courts, there was never any question but that the schooling they should and would receive to be 'equal' to what was generally on offer. It was in fact because 'separate' was proved not to be 'equal' that the case for integration was won. It is, therefore, taken for granted in the USA that all children should attend the same kind of school, receive the same kind of curriculum and graduate with a high school diploma comparable from one school to another.

However, since schools are supported by taxes, raised locally as well as by the State, obviously the schools in the wealthy suburbs bear little resemblance to those of the inner cities. Parents are increasingly aware of this, and recently there has been much adverse comment about the public school system with many parents (up to 50 per cent) saying that they would prefer to use the private, mainly parochial, schools.

Egalitarianism is also basic to the legal system in the USA. Americans are educated through their constitution to be aware of their civil rights. In large numbers they are seemingly quite prepared to go to court and use the due process of the law to get equality i.e. what they hold themselves or their children to be entitled to. They do so to a degree and in ways relatively uncommon even in the developed countries in the West. Interestingly, most of the improvements made through federal legislation for the blacks and the handicapped originated in private and class action suits taken through the judicial system.

The educational and social service system within the USA potentially has the resources, the commitment and the legal procedures which together should ensure the effective delivery of educational services to the population as a whole. As in most other systems, however, the UK included, in the USA poor people meet many stumbling blocks in their attempts to get services. This is a complicated issue and due to many factors, including the inability of the social and protective services, shaped as they are by a combination of statutory, private and professional interests, to work quickly or in cooperation with the range of agencies which could be involved in any one case. Such 'clients' find these public agencies unresponsive, bureaucratic, depersonalised and quite repressive. Many professionals see their function as one of not rocking the boat, as 'problem' assuaging rather than of empowering clients to get access to the range of services available, and thus being enabled to take responsibility for making their own decisions as to what services they need. Consequently, this population can and does develop a real 'dependency' mentality. They see their situation as hopeless and feel empty and isolated. Commenting on the reluctance of some young women to leave a notorious welfare hotel in Manhattan, a community worker, Robert Hayes, points out in the *New York Times*, 14 September 1988, that: 'If you go a little bit deeper, you realise that for them hell has become a familiar cocoon. It's a subtle and more insidious harm that has been done to them than just living with rats and broken pipes'. They lack direction and have not experienced the benefits of cooperation or collective action. They are willing, even eager, to accept help but do not see it as possible that they can help themselves or anyone else. They call for a 'kid-glove' treatment and at the same time are disabled by it. To a limited extent they learn how to manipulate the system, succeed sometimes in the short term but generally lose out in the end. They do not rate themselves as respectable or 'credit worthy' (very important within the American system). They do not have much time left in their lives for aspiration or even feelings and because of the generally chaotic way in which they lead their lives, they are quite often unavailable to their own children and unable to pursue any concerted course of action (e.g. making good use of the social services) which might begin to meet their concerns and alleviate their problems.

Finally, the USA is the classic free enterprise society where 'money talks' and it is normal to measure success in terms of financial rewards. Education is seen almost as a service to commerce and industry and where the State has opted out, as in the case of normal pre-school children, it is quite acceptable that provision will be made by private corporation, for example 'Mary Moppet's Day Care Schools', or, if you have more intellectual aspirations 'Les Petites Academies', two very successful companies whose profits reflect a good return on the initial investment. New York City Department of Health and Day Care Head-Start programs, although supported by substantial sums of public money, are managed and delivered by semi-private concerns though the funding bodies do exercise some control as far as personnel and facilities are concerned.

Pre-School Education

Pre-school provision is patchy and gives cause for concern. 'The lack of quality day care, particularly for infants and toddlers, is another extremely serious situation. As more and more women join the labor force and legislation is passed to put welfare mothers to work, the daily care of the nation's young children is likely to become more chaotic before it becomes less so' (Stokes, 1988).

The system in the New York Metropolitan area, which comprises the five boroughs of New York City (Manhattan), Brooklyn, Queens, Staten Island and the Bronx is as follows. There has been until recently no statutory provision for pre-schoolers, including those who are disabled through handicap, learning difficulties, poverty, social conditions, etc. Pre-school services for handicapped children do exist, however, but in the main have been provided by hospitals or by non-profit making private companies run as businesses by individuals or voluntary organisations incorporated into chartered companies. Up till now these companies have been funded by a combination of State and City money. This is done through a complicated process which involves:

(a) an annual multi-disciplinary assessment of the child;
(b) assigning the child to a specific category of handicap;

(c) submitting a 'case' for the need for special services for scrutiny by professionals attached to the Board of Education;

(d) making a 'case' to the local Family Court who 'officially' determine the child's right to special services;

(e) passing all documentation to the appropriate authorities who then pay out the annual fees due in respect of the child.

Interestingly, this system provides a service to children and their families which is free to those who need it. It is, however, a bureaucratic and time-consuming system for those who are involved in the administration of the programmes, but, at best, is extremely generous by UK standards. Generally there is money for a good staff/student ratio, related services, resources, outings, transport, etc.

While accountability is on the increase, attention has, up till very recently, been concentrated on financial accounts, fire and building regulations and staff criminal records. (This last occasioned by some pre-school sexual abuse cases, well publicised over the last few years). Supervision of the quality of teaching and learning, as could be predicted, has generally been done through quantifiable behavioural norms assessed psychometrically and reported statistically. There is little in the way of centralised curricular guidance in the form of official guidelines, reports or consultative documents. Conferences and seminars tend to be run for profit, by large institutions such as hospitals or the highly commercialised organisations such as the Council for Exceptional Children. Staff Development is seen as a responsibility of the individual companies, and corporations. The best 'programs' have blazed the trail and are extremely good, well-resourced and staffed with a good in-service programme for staff. As the Ford Foundation (1985) points out, these schools 'can (and do) contribute by showing which approaches are most successful, by disseminating information about these findings and by generally informing the debate on how best to counteract the poverty that now significantly impairs future prospects for many of this country's children'. The worst are problematic and do not meet the needs of the children and families concerned.

Early Intervention

Despite the lack of federal or state provision as such, early intervention services for disadvantaged and handicapped children in the USA have received widespread scrutiny over the past twenty years.

Over the years well-documented research has provided overwhelming evidence of the success of early intervention programmes in improving the capacity of pre-school children (Bereiter and Engelman, 1966; Weikart, 1967; Bronfenbrenner; 1975, 1977; Sameroff and Chandler, 1975; Clarke and Clarke, 1976; Field, 1980; Field and Widmayer, 1980; Rutter, 1981; Greenspan, 1981, 1987; Bricker, Bailey and Bruder, 1984; Honig, 1984; Woodhead, 1985). The accepted view arising from this body of research in the USA is that children participating in pre-school programmes show significant increases in cognitive, motor and social skills, as evidenced by the achievement of a high percentage of the goals identified in the Individualised Educational Plans. Parents have reported high levels of satisfaction with their childrens' development as a result of their participation in pre-school programmes, the only question being the extent to which these gains and benefits can be maintained once the child has left the pre-school environment.

Following on the large scale 'investment' in Head Start, numerous studies were undertaken to analyse the longer term effects of early intervention on disadvantaged children, Swann, 1980; Casto, White, 1985; Anastasiow, 1986; Casto and Mastropieri, 1986. These studies showed that while initial gains in IQ were not maintained, the experimental groups outscored control groups on tests of achievement and showed, on average, less need of special education services. They were reported as more strongly committed to schooling and rated themselves higher than comparable controls.

Writing up a famous on-going study of poor 3 year olds Zigler and Berman (1983), comment that those enrolled in the early 1960's were later more likely to finish high school, land jobs and avoid crime and avoid teenage pregnancy. Relevant also is the fact that recently the scores of minority students seeking admission to college have improved. Donald Stewart, President of the College Board, attributes this gain to early intervention programmes such as Head Start. (*New York Times*, 20 September 1988).

In 1971 an important research book reporting a study by Werner, Burman and French demonstrated that many perinatal problems could be alleviated by a supportive environment. In a multi-racial sample of 670 infants, born on the Hawaiian Island of Kuai, all groups of children, regardless of race, social class or age of mother had about the same proportion of perinatal complications. In this sample 13 per cent suffered complications and 3 per cent suffered severe complications. It was, however, group membership which predicted how well the infant recovered from the complication. Children born into lower income families were less likely to recover fully by age 2. By age 10 the effect of perinatal problems had all but disappeared for all the groups, but children from lower income groups had lower scores on IQ tests and were doing worse in school than children from middle income groups.

An extensive body of research supports these findings e.g. Sameroff and Chandler, 1975; Garber and Heber, 1979; Greenspan, 1981, 1987; Guralnick and Bennett, 1987. In general the most stressful the environment – when parents lack economic and social support systems – the more likely it will be that infants will not recover quickly form perinatal risk factors. However, if there are adequate economic resources, if the parents are not under psychological stress and if the infant is born normal except for perinatal complications, the effects do not usually last. These authors talk about the infants' buffering against difficulties of early adjustment and the infant's self righting ability. Given any kind of appropriate, responsive environment, perinatal complications are less likely to create lasting deficits.

Single stresses such as an accident or injury or illness are rarely associated with long term disorder. Yet any multiple stresses against a background of economic disadvantage consistently lead to negative outcomes. Early malnutrition, it is claimed, has an effect on achievement and performance in intellligence tests, though most studies support the view that malnutrition acts in concert with many other factors to produce its effect.

It has, therefore, been generally borne out by research, that in the USA there are many young children, pre-schoolers and infants particularly, suffering from the adverse effects of poverty and disadvantage, when at the same time there is substantial evidence of the ameliorating effects of early intervention; that if and when multi-risk families are given the kind of early intervention which can help them and their 'definitely at risk' children, good results are possible (Greenspan 1981, 1987).

As Stokes writes

At present it is purely an accident of geography, family dynamics and income, and professional networks whether a baby who has been in intensive care is followed up for possible developmental delays, whether or not a small child is immunised against the major childhood diseases: whether or not a child's father or mother is able to find social support and advice when the ordinary crises of child rearing arise or whether or not signs that a home environment is becoming severely abusive or neglectful are recognised before a child comes to hospital with injuries (Stokes, 1988).

Policy and Legislation

It is clear that the Federal Government is concerned about this disparity between the public intention and the individual reality and is quite serious in its intentions to improve the special services available to handicapped children through the recent legislation framed under EHA (Assistance to States for Education of Handicapped Children).

The purpose of this new legislation (PL99.457, Federal Register, Vol. 52 No. 222, November 1987) is to provide financial assistance to States:

(a) to develop and implement a statewide comprehensive, coordinated, multi-disciplinary, interagency program of early intervention services for infants and toddlers with handicaps and their families;
(b) to facilitate the coordination of payment for early intervention services from Federal, State, local and private sources (including public and private insurance coverage); and
(c) to enhance the States' capacity to provide quality early intervention services and improve existing early intervention services being provided to infants and toddlers with handicaps and to their families.

This new Federal Law will require States to define the 'at-risk' pre-school population, provide a local/statewide directory of services and specify a timetable for provision. So States now must get answers to the following questions: Who is to be helped? What services are to be offered? How quickly can all of this be organised and put in place?

They will also be charged to produce proper procedures for the identification and evaluation of the 'at risk' infants and toddlers through a programme designed to raise public awareness, to implement a comprehensive 'child find' system and ensure the improvement of the existing procedures designed to identify, locate and evaluate all handicapped children, particularly infants and toddlers.

While some of these procedures have been in operation since PL94.142, the new legislation has clearly been affected by research findings which have shown that much of the initial early intervention produced by that legislation was rather narrowly conceived in terms of educational and cognitive goals, neglecting a holistic view of the child as a member of a family and a community, and with a unique cultural identity and social background.

The new legislation has come to grips with the issues which arise from this kind of awareness, through the requirement to produce an Individualised Family Service Plan (IFSP), and in the design and intention of the Procedural Safeguards. These IFSPs are based in part on the Individualised Educational Plans (IEPs) formerly prescribed. While there are some similarities between these two provisions there are also some distinct differences. The content of the IFSP is more comprehensive and includes components that go well beyond the scope of the IEP. The IFSP, under the new law must contain statements relating to the child's present levels of development in the areas of cognition, speech/language, psychosocial, motor and self-help, the family's strengths and needs and how these will inhibit or enhance the child's development.

States must also detail the major outcomes to be achieved for child and family, as opposed to an Individualised Educational Program (IEP). They must also specify the criteria, procedures and timelines for determining progress and the early intervention services which will be provided to meet the unique needs of the child and family. Further, they must specify the intensity, frequency and method of service, and give the specific dates for the initiation and duration of services, and the name of the case manager. Interestingly, and in keeping with the intention to mainstream, they must also describe the procedures which have been taken to facilitate the transition of the child into mainstream education.

The Procedural Safeguards involve the State in procedures specifically designed to protect and enhance the role to be played by parents. They must set up hearing, appeal and review procedures and produce a 'timely' resolution of complaints. States must conduct the hearing of the complaints in the native language of the family and at a time convenient to parents. Parents must get access to *all* records, and are entitled to confidentiality in all procedures.

Another matter of concern, highlighted formally through research and informally by anyone who has been closely involved with the delivery of special services, is the question of coordination. Many of the parents, overburdened as they are, report their dissatisfaction with career professionals more concerned with their particular specialism than with the coordination of the total array of services. In order to overcome this, the new legislation provides financial assistance to States:

(a) develop and implement a Statewide comprehensive, coordinated and multi-disciplinary interagency program of early intervention services for infants and toddlers with handicaps and their families;
(b) facilitate the coordination of payment for early intervention services from Federal, State, local and private sources;
(c) enhance the States' capacity to provide early intervention services and expand and improve existing early intervention services

being provided to infants and toddlers with handicaps and their families.

This will largely be achieved through the nature and quality of the Case Management Services which are:

Services provided to families of infants and toddlers with handicaps to assist them in gaining access to early intervention services ident-ified in the IFSP.

Clearly, the messages coming from the research previously quoted have been well accepted. This legislation has an unequivocal prescriptive ring about it with its clearly stated intention that a comprehensive range of services will be provided for handicapped children and their families. It is so written that States will find it difficult to evade any aspect of their responsibilities. As such it is consonant with the intention to provide a free and appropriate education and shows the potential power for good that is inherent with the American democratic process dedicated as it is to a public system of education.

The Council for Exceptional Children, however, in a political call sent to members in 1987 asking them to lobby senators and congress members is not too sanguine: The levels of funding in the House for pre-school services to children, ages 3–5, is significantly below the level of funding set out in PL.99.457. ($216 million needed in FY.1988). By not fully funding the new legal requirements, the appropriation bill places in jeop-ardy the 1990 mandate for serving all handicapped children, ages 3–5, and may give a signal to states that the federal government will not meet its financial obligations under the law. The Council continues: 'Funding under the new Part II Program for Infants and Toddlers in the House is also woefully inadequate and may encourage states to reconsider the degree to which they may wish to participate'. It is, however, interesting to note that the Procedural Safeguards, detailed above, reflect an intention to respect parents' rights and responsibilities and their cultural and social identity.

Finally, the development of the 'Case Management Services' shows both awareness of the problems of client access to services and the need to organise in such a way that the clients are liberated and empowered rather than designated as passive recipients of services provided by career professionals.

Now that this law is in place, it is clear that the idea of the IFSP has produced wide-spread controversy and, as could be predicted, a deal of professional anxiety. Many families and service providers alike are concerned, it is claimed, about the potential problems arising from assessment and planning process that will be intrusive, judgmental, static or unresponsive to the family's needs.

However, a more appropriate set of questions for professionals to consider are related to how they will function in a situation where the balance of power may change and success be judged by the extent to which parents have become decision makers trying to take control of their own lives. And the final question, of course, is to what extent any of this will succeed in the end, running counter, as it does, to the broad social forces which seem to be more about containment and service provision by professionals rather than the transformation of society through the empowerment of the poor and oppressed.

The 6/75 Program: History and Development

The '6/75 Program' originated around 1980 in the Kingsbrook Jewish Medical Center, Brooklyn, New York, as a hospital based programme designed to do three things: i.e. to provide on site educational programmes for severely handicapped children in a long stay rehabilitation hospital, in-service programmes for teachers and in-house training for other professional staff in the hospital, all of whom understood care but knew little about the benefits of education. Procedures were also developed in order to identify and assess infants and toddlers with a range of handicaps (often surfacing at the hospital clinics), and to provide them with home teachers who would work with the children and their families in order to support them and thus reduce the risk of long-term hospitalisation.

This private programme has developed and now is multi-disciplinary with teachers, psychologists and therapists employed on a full-time basis in sex education based programmes. While each is designed to meet the needs of a particular group of children, for example language impaired, physically handicapped, behaviourally disturbed etc., the 6/75 group appear in all groups, in numbers disproportionate to the normative nature and degree of their disabilities. Characteristically they can be physically neglected, health impaired, language and learning delayed, and behaviourally disturbed. They often present as 'needy children' the children of mothers who are themselves 'needy children'.

All of the thirty-seven families presently in the 6/75 group had been involved with at least two outside agencies before joining the program. Almost all were receiving financial support from Aid for Families with Dependent Children (AFDC) i.e. they were on welfare, and had been so for most of their lives. Most had food stamps or had had food 'handouts' from the Federal Government under a system for the disposal of surplus foodstuff. Only two mothers had had ten years schooling (despite the national commitment to a twelve year free and appropriate education) and fifteen mothers and twenty fathers were or had been substance users i.e. marijuana, alcohol, heroin and crack. Twenty-two of the mothers had been reported as neglectful or abusive to the extent that the children had been taken into care. Thirteen of the mothers were below age seventeen at the time of the first child's delivery. Most families were living in substandard accommodation and at any one time around five families were homeless and living in 'welfare hotels', a misnomer of some proportion.

Of the sixty children involved, fourteen were multiply handicapped as a result of pre-natal problems including drug and alcohol abuse. Fifteen were reported as 'failure to thrive' and were below the fifth percentile in height and weight. Fourteen were emotionally disturbed due to neglect and/or abusive treatment; seven were premature and born into very poor families. Six had chromosomal or genetic disorders, most of which could have been identified in utero. Eight were specifically diagnosed as having problems related to drug and alcohol abuse. Six had developmental delays due to neglect, allergies and abuse and seven had severe behavioural difficulties due to the same reasons.

These children and their families therefore present a complex array of difficulties which act and interact to be profoundly disabling, but which research shows are not incurable in the physical sense or irremediable in terms of care and education. Left without support, however, their life chances are poor. Traditionally this is the population who find it almost impossible to break out of the cycle of poverty and in later life tend to occupy an undue proportion of places in hospitals and prisons.

The *New York Times*, 3 September 1986, reports: 'New York City will soon face "medical gridlock" unless hospitals add hundreds of new beds, and out patient clinics and drug abuse clinics are rapidly expanded, particularly in poor areas. A study 'New York City's Hospital Occupancy Crisis: Caring for a Changing Population' concluded that a dramatic increase in urban poverty and its consequences, particularly drug abuse, was the main factor in rising hospital occupancy rates.'

The following extracts from a series of longer Case Studies produced by the 6/75 Program give an account of the lives and problems of some of the children and their families, as they come to the programme.

1 Isadora S., Robert., Eduardo and Julie

'Ms L., the social worker from the Special Services, who brought Isadora S told us that she was well-known to the agency. Her 17 and 19 years old sons, Jose and Antonio had been placed in residential treatment centres for the emotionally and socially maladjusted. At the time she had living with her Julie (5 years), Roberto (3½ years) and Eduardo (10 months).

When Isadora and her three children arrived, they were a pitiful sight. The baby was wrapped in a thin worn blanket, filthy and full of holes. The other children were thin, smelly and unkempt. Roberto needed a diaper change, but Isadora only saw fit to change him after urging by the social worker and the psychologist. She did not wash him though he was crying with a nasty rash. Eduardo was so weak that effectively he had no way of expressing his needs. Julie, who appeared brighter and who was interested in the toys, cried inconsolably when she was taken away.

Isadora's ways were indicative of an extremely disturbed individual. She had little self-monitoring or social ability. She could be heard from a long way off whenever she came to visit, yelling at the children and continuing to slap them without change of pace. Most of the time the children were clamouring for something to eat but rarely got anything other than potato chips or candy. Her anger spilled out during every interaction and undid the relationship which the team were trying to create. A call asking her to meet her children from school would cause her to curse and scream. When things went wrong she always had a ready excuse that it was not her fault.

When asked to plan so that help could be provided, she refused to cooperate. There was no one that she felt she could trust, not even in her family. This was not paranoia but an acceptance of the harsh and brutal events of her daily life. Her children's father was reported as wanting to kill her; her older sons (Antonio and Jose) had said the same and there was a protection order, at one time, preventing them from going home or molesting Isadora. Her neighbours were heavily involved in drugs and crime. She did not believe that the authorities would do her any good and felt that they were interested in taking the children away.

During the time that the children were on the Program, Antonio and Jose came back to live with Isadora. It was typical of her confusion that, despite the protection order, intermittently she fought with the police to allow them to stay with her. Antonio and Jose got into a car thieving ring, directing operations from the family 'home'. Their activities were reported to the police but got scant attention in an area where the drug related homicide rate had jumped by 15 per cent in the last year alone.

Roberto, age 5, could name and value various cars and years, talked about killing people to get their cars and was used as a runner by his older brothers. Roberto had been training the family dog (whom he claimed had 'special powers') to lunge at people, especially his mother, but was himself finally savaged by the dog. Antonio and Jose finally left, leaving

Isadora again without financial support. Roberto was devastated that his mother had 'let them go'.

Social Services, who had judged Isadora to be retarded and disturbed, decided to make a lump sum payment for furniture etc., which amounted to $5,000. Within a week, this money had been taken by Antonio to support his now expensive drug habit.

Initially Roberto, having witnessed many brutal fights was threatening to the other children in the program, while Eduardo was in constant motion as if in flight, his powers of concentration poor and his language abusive. The other children called them the 'gorillas'.

The children improved but the family situation continued to deteriorate with the elder brothers out and in constantly. Eduardo had blisters that could only have come from cigarette burns. Isadora became more confused and abusive. Eduardo was admitted for three months residential care and made satisfactory progress. In school Roberto was pleased to eat his fill, take warm baths and have caring teachers who helped him considerably.

Eventually, despite a considerable expenditure of time and effort, the decision was made that the well-being of the children was being fundamentally threatened by Isadora and her two older boys. The younger children were by this time in reasonable shape, physically, educationally and in terms of their behavioural and social adjustment. Interestingly it was the children themselves who 'reported' Isadora. In the end they were handed over, by the program, to the Child Protection Services, a decision which was felt to be inescapable at the time, but from which little comfort could be drawn.'

2 Hetty, Tommy, Sammy and Faith

'Hetty was sent to the program by order of the Brooklyn Supervision District Attorney, having been given five years probation for child homicide. Her oldest daughter had died at age 3, as a result of neglect and malnutrition, and the youngest, Sammy, had almost died of dehydration and 'failure to thrive'. Hetty herself had (undiagnosed) low blood pressure and diabetes and had, in fact, at the point at which the eldest child had died of meningitis and general lack of care, slept for two whole days without waking up.

She was required by the Court to be in treatment and training and came to the program through the auspices of a foster agency with an excellent record of collaboration. Soon after this the fourth child, Faith, was born and immediately placed in foster care.

Hetty was helped to understand that none of her children could be given back to her without a good showing on her part, and in fact the criminal charges would continue to be held against her if she did not cooperate and conform to the demands of the probation order. She was not, in fact, married to the father of the children (he had already a wife and children). He gave her no support, financial or emotional, and told the case worker that he was not interested in Hetty or the children.

Hetty was supported for five years through the program. Although there were ups and downs, she began to seize the opportunities offered and ask for the help she needed. The professionals in the program conveyed to Hetty their belief in her potential as a responsible provider and care giver even when, from time to time, she failed to show-up for workshops or training sessions.

Housing was a great problem and, in fact, there were times when blind bureaucracy had Hetty in a 'no win' situation. She had to be settled in housing before she could have the children back but could not be given housing because her children were in care! It was through the intervention of the program, in particular the social worker who took the case back to the court, that this particular double bind was eventually resolved. Although her ability was borderline and she could not write or count properly, in the end she met all the demands as far as the management of her life was concerned. She continued to want her children, despite the fact that the eldest, Tommy was very difficult at home and in school.

After the completion of her probation and the attached conditions, the children were due to be returned to Hetty. Unfortunately Tommy's behaviour was such that he had been moved from one foster home to another. Lacking the support previously supplied by the program he became quite abusive and probably Hetty will continue to need some support from outside agencies if she is going to be able to keep him with her.'

3 Tanya, James, Leroy, Arthur and Lorrie

'When Tanya first came to us at aged 17, with three children including one set of twins, she had been black-balled by all the other agencies with whom she had dealings. She had a well-deserved reputation as a trouble maker. She had blamed the hospital where the children had been born for the fact that the twins were somewhat handicapped. She took the landlord to court for stealing, when in fact she owed him rent money. She accused the judge of racial prejudice when he dismissed her claim.

When one of the twins died, probably due to neglect brought about by her addiction to marijuana, and she was under suspicion, she enlisted strong local political support and again accused the 'accusers' of racism against her. She was suffering from a virulent form of gonorrhea, had not told 'Junior', the father of the children, and had infected him. She had been thrown out of one apartment after another for non-payment of rent, having habitually spent her allowances on other things, mainly herself.

Despite her many shortcomings, Tanya had a lot of spunk. She was not unintelligent, and was prepared to fight for herself and her children. Somehow or other she had kept some sort of vision as to what she and her children might become. She had a sensible and supportive mother even though Tanya had tried her patience beyond belief. Through the program she was given a home-maker, Jessie, who had the right combination of qualities for Tanya. Jessie was hard-working and had very definite standards about how the home should be cared for. She was not frightened of Tanya, stood no nonsense and could keep a grip on her. Jessie never despaired or give up despite many ups and downs.

Soon after she joined us, Tanya had her fourth child, a girl called Lorrie. The children settled well in the program. Leroy, the surviving twin, looked as if he was carrying the world on his shoulders and had to be separated from his brother for whom he clearly felt responsible. Tanya expected too much of him and had to be told clearly, that it was wrong to use him as a substitute father, 'Junior' having departed the scene.

Tanya responded well, if somewhat fitfully, to the way the program was run. She liked all the social gatherings, seven per year, turned up pretty regularly to workshops, parties etc., though she sometimes left the team with the feeling that she was 'interviewing' them, rather than the other way about.

She was, however, one of those people who have to hit bottom before they can come up. On account of her total unreliability with money (though it should be remembered that she was still not twenty) she lost all possibility of getting an apartment to rent and ended up in a 'welfare' hotel in Manhattan. This was altogether a shocking place, unsafe and unsanitary. While in a way it was her pride and inability to take help that got her there, it was the same qualities which got her out less than a year later, into an apartment of her own and with a steady job.

The style of working in the program really suited Tanya. She was never patronised; she did not get the 'kid glove' treatment and learned quickly not to expect it. Her problems were not solved for her. Rather she was given an entry into a world where through using her head, she could begin to work out solutions to her own problems. Tanya respected the professionals she worked with in the 6/75 Program, at the same time as she despised those who undermined her through their devaluation of her as a person, particularly the School Board, teachers, and social workers.

Examples of this can be seen from her attempts first of all to 'claim' for the child who had died by getting Leroy, his twin, to double up for him, and secondly her claim that Leroy had arthritis (which he had not) so that she could get a special allowance for him. She is now, five years on, reasonably settled, with her children well-cared for and in regular attendance at school – a long way from the visit made to her in a dark and filthy apartment in a Brooklyn slum!'

The Programme

The goal of the programme is to provide conditions where parents, professionals and para-professionals can share their information, knowledge and skills with each other. For this process to work there has to be a willingness to build a team, an interest in each other, and the ability to learn the skills and techniques used by all the others in the team, including parents. This is done as follows.

Regularly throughout the year, each member of the team, including the teacher, presents workshops designed to extend the knowledge and skills of the other team members, and the parents. At these workshops each member must demonstrate in action what he/she assesses and discuss the implications for children and families.

The specific aim of this way of working is 'role extension'. In other words it is a serious attempt to break down the sterile demarcation disputes and professional barriers characteristic of many such 'programs'. Team members were helped to define their roles and responsibilities more precisely. Parents and professionals acquired realistic expectations of what each had to contribute. The procedures went a long way to reduce role ambiguity and confusion, popularly acknowledged sources of much of the conflict which bedevils team working. In addition, these procedures made staff very aware of redundancy and decreased the number of times the child and the family were assessed on the same or similar items.

The model for screening and placement was called an 'Arena Evaluation', and was derived from work done at other federally funded 'programs' (Eagen, Petise and Toole, 1980).

A preliminary interview lasting around one hour includes the parent, the referring agency (if there is one) and all members of the team. Children are assessed using an *ad hoc* selection of the formal and informal procedures used by each professional. The atmosphere is quite informal and the parents are invited to comment at all stages of the procedures – and often do! The parents are also shown a video of the program. Coffee and Danish pastries are available (and demolished). Interestingly enough, the parents are not over-awed by the situation because, instead of the spotlight being on them as it would be in a one-to-one interview, quite often they were simply observing or listening to the views of the team without being expected to make immediate responses. In effect the procedures gave them more time and space to absorb what was going on, and to do so more successfully than they would through one-to-one interviews.

The main advantages noted are over time as follows:

(a) The arena assessment in effect cut out redundancy in 'testing'. This was important for parents and children.

(b) In the company of their peers, the professionals were better prepared and aware of how they were 'coming over'.

(c) Professionals were specific and focused.

(d) All team members and parents who had seen and heard each other's procedures gained additional knowledge about the child as a whole.

(e) The comments of the parents provided a 'valid' and valuable source of information; they were received in context and were stimulated by the variety of activities demonstrated. Generally they were not constrained and the information they provided covered many aspects of the child's functioning.

A meeting is held immediately after and a group decision made about whether or not to offer a place. Priorities are established and a hypothesis developed as to what would be an appropriate programme for the child.

After the children have been assessed, as described as above, and a tentative program developed, team members continue to work in cooperation with teachers and parents. The level of involvement and the amount of time that parents are expected to spend is very definitely negotiated with the parents (mainly the mothers). Most of them already have too many demands on their time. They are, in the main, overburdened by the conditions of their lives and the last thing they need is for the programme to engender feelings of guilt that they are not 'good' mothers, because they are not prepared to spend a lot of time in the school, mainly, of course, at a time which suits the school organisation but not their particular timetables.

The educational program developed by the teacher, in consultation with the other team members, is closely monitored, with all 'consultants' encouraged to discuss, suggest, modify etc. with the aim of improving the program. The teacher, however, remains the key, always aware of the range of needs of the child as they relate to his/her total development. Each team member is expected to practise role release, to share their knowledge and skills, to 'train' the others and monitor their work in an open and cooperative way.

Among the advantages reaped from this approach to services are those that:

(a) Each team member, including the parents, gains an understanding of the other's philosophy, style, and abilities.

(b) The teacher plays a central role in the process of getting to know the child and the family.

(c) The clinical staff become an integral part of the process of teaching and learning.

(d) The parent is enabled to make a significant and valued contribution to the process of teaching/learning.

(e) Time is managed efficiently.

(f) There is very little formal testing as such, while information regarding the child's learning style and abilities increases considerably.

(g) A classroom-centered approach to teaching and therapy allows a child to learn in a child-centered environment.

(h) All members of the team, including parents, begin to learn from each other.

Evaluation

Clearly, the evaluation of a program of this nature cannot be done using an experimental, empirical research design. Ethical and legal considerations preclude the use of a control group, and therefore it was decided to use an action research methodology where information was gathered over the years from a number of sources. This included teachers' records based on structured observation, videos, case studies, field notes, diaries, interviews, analytic memos, oral histories and informal conversations.

In order to get some kind of objectivity, the results obtained were looked at in comparison with the literature about comparable groups and convergent validity was used i.e. comparable information was gathered from a variety of sources, each of which was asked to address similar outcomes. This proved to be both informative and enlightening to all concerned, particularly the parents who had rarely had access to this level of information and debate.

Within the limitations of this kind of study, the following results are presented with a reasonable degree of confidence.

Families

One sixth of the families were either 'lost' or had still serious problems (e.g. Isadora). Five-sixths showed some degree of improvement i.e. they were settled in homes, at work or training, attending a drug programme, or attending hospital clinics regularly with their children, the last being a good indicator of family well-being (e.g. Hetty).

One third showed continuous, consistent progress in terms of having more control over the conditions of their lives. These families and children rarely required special services outside of those normally provided and those which they did have were more related to specific educational needs such as speech/physical therapy, as opposed to the general range of social and protective services (e.g. Tanya).

Children

Out of the sixty children, forty-nine showed a definite improvement across a number of dimensions, including their physical well being, school placement and progress, and were considered to be in a consistent caring home environment. Twenty-five were regarded as making good to excellent progress. Twenty were in mainstream schools and kindergartens, and while this is a lower figure than that reported in some studies, those who were there, were reported as having 'positive attitudes' to school. Almost all of the children showed improved scores in language, cognitive and motor functioning and were rated more highly in social skills than would have been expected from their earlier levels of performance.

In reviewing the findings, the effectiveness of the program becomes fairly evident. While the limitation of the research design must be considered, the positive nature of the results indicate that the 6/75 Program has had some beneficial and lasting effects upon its 'graduates' and their families. It looks, for example, as if the programme, with its particular attitudes to parental/professional collaboration, is facilitating the placement of disadvantaged and handicapped children in mainstream schools and classes and, more importantly, helping them to stay there. While the follow-up data indicated that only one-third of the total number of children involved were assigned to and placed in regular education, this represented a high proportion of those who came from the 6/75 group and had no other handicap. Most of these children are now progressing through the grades without being held back and are requiring no additional services outside of those routinely provided in the classroom. Teachers' ratings indicate that in comparison with their peers, these children are performing and socialising well and have extremely positive attitudes to school and to learning.

It seems as if participation in the 6/75 Program has helped a good proportion of the families involved, with all their difficulties, to cope better with the difficult circumstances of their lives, circumstances which are not likely to change measurably for the better in the foreseeable future. They have been encouraged and supported to return to education, finish school, some to start college and get themselves into the world of work. The whole experience has helped them to be more effective parents to the children they have, while at the same time encouraging them to postpone subsequent pregnancies until they are older or more mature and better able to make a more conscious choice about their lives. This has become crucial at a time when crack is freely available and one 'hit' can cause grave damage to the developing foetus. They have been encouraged to leave the desolate, depressing and dangerous public and private housing, which to too many seems to be the norm, and to seek out for themselves, a more stable and benign environment.

Finally, there is little doubt that it is within the capacity of the USA, with all its resources, to save many of these children and mothers at risk. It cannot, however, be done by piecemeal proposals or goodwill campaign gestures. It requires political will as well as policy commitment. As Senator Moynihan writes (*New York Times*, 25 September 1988): 'From almost the moment that the "dual family" system appeared, successive Congresses and Presidents have tried to respond . . . Often we have come close but, so far, always we have failed. The central reason is that we have only slowly come to recognise and accept the new social reality we are dealing with.'

The present welfare legislation, and this will include PL.99.457, with all of its requirements and procedures, tries to address this reality. 'If we fail this time', Moynihan concludes, 'it will be something American society can't handle. Which means we will have spoiled the next century.'

References

Anastasiow, N. J. (1979) 'Current Issues in Child Development' in Simmonds A. and Martin (Eds) *International Conference on Parents and Young Children*, New York, Grunel and Stratton.

Bereiter, C. and Engelmann, S. (1966) *The effectiveness of direct instructional performance and achievement in reading and arithmetic*, Champaign IL. Academic Preschool – ERIC. ED030 496.

Bricker, D., Bailey and Bruder, M. B. (1984) 'The efficacy of early intervention and the handicapped infant: A wise or wasted resource', in Wotraich M. and

Routh, D. K. (Eds). *Advances in development and behavioural pediatrics*, 67 pp. 45–46.

Bronfenbrenner, U. (1975) 'Is Early Intervention Effective?', in Frielander, B. L. Sternett, G. M. Kirk, G. E. (Eds) *Exceptional Infant*, 3, pp. 449–475, New York, Brunner/Mazel.

Bronfenbrenner, U. (1977) 'Towards and experimental ecology of human development', *American Psychologist*, 32, pp. 513–531.

Casto, G. and Mastropieri, M. A. (1986) 'The efficacy of early intervention programs: A meat-analysis, *Exceptional Children*, 52, pp. 417–424.

Casto, G. and White, K. (1985) 'The efficacy of early intervention programs with environmentally at risk infants', in Frank, M. (Ed) *Infant intervention programs: Truth and untruths*, New York, Haworth Press, pp. 37–50.

Clarke, A. M. and Clarke, A. D. B. (1976) *Early Experience, Myth and Evidence*, New York, Free Press.

Eagen, C. S., Petise, K. and Toole, A. L. (1980) *The Trandisciplinary Training Assessment and Consultation Model, Yorktown Heights*, New York Board of Cooperative Education Services.

Field, T. H., Widmayer, S., Stringer, S. and Ignatoff, E. (1980) 'Teenage lower class black mothers and their pre-term infants: An intervention and developmental follow-up' *Child Development*, 51, pp. 426–436.

Field, T. M. (1982) 'Infants born at risk: Early compensatory strategies' in Bond L. and Joffee J. (Eds), *Facilitating infant and early childhood development* Burlington, Vermont University of Vermont Press.

Ford Foundation (1985) *Women and Children and Poverty in America*, New York, Ford Foundation.

Garber, H. and Heber, R. (1981) 'The efficacy of early intervention with family rehabilitation' in Begab, M., Haywood, H. C. and Garber, H. L. (Eds), *Psycho-social influences in retarded performance*, Baltimore, University Park Press.

Guralnick, N. J. and Bennett, F. C. *The effectiveness of early intervention for at-risk and handicapped children*, New York Academic Press.

Honig, A. S. (1984) 'Reflections on infant intervention programs: What have we learned?', *Children in Contemporary Society*, 17, pp. 81–92.

House of Representatives Select Committee (1987) *Children, Youth and Families*, Washington DC, US Govt. printing Office.

Rutter, M. (1981) 'The long term effects of early experience', *Developmental Medicine and Child Neurology*, 22, pp. 800–815.

Rutter, M. (1981) 'Stress coping and development: Some issues and questions', *Journal of Child Psychology and Psychiatry*, 22, pp. 323–356.

Schorr, D. and L. (1988) *Within Our Reach: Breaking the Cycle of Disadvantage and Despair*, New York, Doubleday/Anchor.

Sameroff, A. J. and Chandler, M. J. (1975) 'Reproductive risk and the continuum of caretaking casualty', in Horowitz, F. D. (Ed) *Review of Child Development Research*, Chicago, University of Chicago Press.

Stokes, E. (1988) Editorial in *Infants and Young Children*, 1,.

Swann, W. W. (1980) 'The Handicapped Children's Early Education Program', *Exceptional Children*, 47, pp. 12–16.

Tobier, E. (1984) *The Changing Face of Poverty: Trends in New York City's population in poverty*, (1960–1990), New York, Community Service Society.

Tomlinson, S. (1987) 'Why Johnny Can't Read', in *European Journal of Special Educational Needs*, 3, 1.

Weikart, D. P. (1967) *Pre-school intervention: Preliminary results of the Perry Pre-school Project*, Ann Arbor, Michigan, Campus Publishers.

Woodhead, M. (1985) 'Pre-school education has long-term effects: But can they be generalised?', *Oxford Review of Education*, 11, pp. 133–155.

Werner, E. Burman, J. and French, F. (1971) *The Children of Kuai*, Honolulu, University of Hawaii Press.

Zigler, E., and Berman, W. (1983) Discerning the Future of Early Childhood Intervention *American Psychologist*, 38, pp. 894–906.

Chapter Seven

Rehabilitation Development in South West Asia:[1] Conflicts and Potentials

M. Miles

A Fresh Look

During the International Year of the Child (1979) many Asian countries began to review their rehabilitation services for people with disabilities. Impetus was added by the International Year of Disabled Persons (1981). Many schemes and projects were started as the Decade of Disabled Persons 1983–1992 was launched (UN CSDHA, 1983a).

Rehabilitation development in some ways paralleled health service development, following a professional/institutional model in the modern urban sector, influenced by European practice from the 1930s to 1960s; while people needing help in the rural areas and urban slums derived modest benefit from traditional practitioners and family/neighbourhood efforts and adaptations, with minimal input of modern knowledge, method or technology.

Efforts to survey the extent of need for rehabilitation services were hampered by inadequacies of conceptual development – the difficulty of reaching appropriate 'official' definitions of disability in all its varying degrees, as recordable by an observer, was compounded by a lack of familiarity with the realities of life as experienced by people with disabilities. Here, rehabilitation development has been slower and more difficult than health development.

Concepts and meanings of health and sickness and attitudes towards sick or healthy people vary considerably between different societies but in general seem to be at both a more developed and more widely accessible level than are concepts of disability. In planning and policy development, these conceptual inadequacies and unfamiliarities have a considerable effect, though the source may not be apparent.

The processes of policy formation in Asia, on what is considered a minor social welfare concern, are far from obvious and are difficult to document. To *have* a formulated disability policy is a recent notion. To consult the concerned constituency and to develop and revise policy with public participation is a process with which Asian governments are unfamiliar. The views expressed here derive from personal experience of rehabilitation development in private and Government sectors in Pakistan, and exchanges among a network of colleagues in Asian countries in the 1980s.

Demographic background and baseline

Ten years ago India, Pakistan and Bangladesh had a combined population of about 850 million, growing at around 2.5 per cent per annum. In 1988 the population is about 1,000 million, growing by at least 20 million per annum. Perspective on the problems facing national planners may be gained by sketching[2] the prospects of a random 1,000 live neonates who should have reached their fifth birthday in respectively 1979 and 1988 (See Table 1).

Table 1: Neonate's Life Prospects

	1979	1988
Still alive on fifth birthday	800	850
Immunised against polio	50	400
Having noticeable disability (3 per cent level)	24	26
Enrolling in primary school	500	700
Enrolling in primary school with noticeable disability	10	14
Will proceed to secondary school	200	275
To secondary school with noticeable disability	4	5

The 2 per cent of enrolled pupils who have perceived disabilities (Miles, 1985a) are 'casually' integrated, with little attention paid to their problems. Where primary school enrolment is around 70 per cent, more than half of whom leave before completing primary education, the handful of disabled pupils sink or swim by their own efforts.

The number of rehabilitation institutions and organisations may also be compared across approximately a decade (see Table 2).

To make such comparisons may suggest that the plan was to increase formal facilities, which in the 1970s might indeed have been the case. By the mid 1980s, community-orientated strategies were attracting attention,

Table 2: Rehabilitation Institutions and Organisations

	1975	1978	1986
India	836[1]		8000[2]
Pakistan	55[3]		127[3]
Bangladesh		21[4]	78[5]

Sources:
1 Nimbkar, 1975
2 Narasimhan and Mukherjee, 1986
3 Directorate General of Special Education, 1986
4 Ahmadullah *et al*, 1981
5 Gazi, 1986

so that some of the resources shown in Table 3 (which by their nature are seldom reliably quantified) should also be inspected.

Table 3: Community Resources

	1979	1988
Families active in home rehabilitation	Some	Some
Disabled adults active in counselling	Few	Few
Local community rehab resource centres	Nil	Few
Primary health workers using some rehab skills	Few	Some
Traditional healers, bonesetters, acupuncturists, etc.	Many	Many
'How-to' rehab manuals in local languages	Nil	Few
Teachers having some inservice training to help disabled pupils in the ordinary classroom	Nil	Few
Self-help associations of disabled people	Nil	Few
Schools with planned mainstreaming	Few	Some

Attitudes and Philosophies

The range of attitudes towards disability and persons with disability in South Asian countries appears to be similar to that reported in the West. Fear, contempt, distaste, distancing, mockery and condemnation, sometimes associated with the idea of divine retribution or *karma*, form the unpleasant end of the spectrum (Miles 1983).

Disability in Asia was first 'labelled' over two thousand years ago. Mentions occur in legal codes, e.g. the laws of Manu in the Indian subcontinent, and the Wang Kih in China, around the second century BC; and in religious codes, e.g. in Muslim and Zoroastrian scriptures of the sixth and seventh centuries AD. Religious beliefs have presumably played some role in forming and maintaining attitudes towards persons with disabilities – for better or for worse.

Determining the effect of religious beliefs is problematical, since there is seldom an authoritative source to pronounce the teaching of any given religion concerning a specific social problem or phenomenon beyond the merely platitudinous. Where there exists a source giving the 'correct' teaching, it may be little known or acknowledged by the ordinary adherents of that religion. Asian religions and ideologies are highly diversified and resistant to Western systematizing – more like an ocean in which to swim than a set of logically coherent belief constructs and ethical systems.

It is sometimes believed that mentally impaired people receive more tolerant treatment in Asia than Europe, though public facilities for the welfare of disabled people are clearly much greater in Europe than in Asia. How far this arises from social development and economic strength, and how far from the prevailing Western political and religious philosophies is unclear. A Western nation noted for its cultural, literary and religious heritage recently implemented a plan for exterminating the chronically sick, epileptic, disabled or retarded persons: an abuse of power for which there is scarcely a parallel in the 'less developed' nations.

One authority on Buddhist ethics (Saddhatissa, 1970) asserts that: 'Buddhism is essentially a mind-culture . . . the importance of being aware of, and controlling, one's thoughts is continually stressed . . . "Mind precedes all things; all things have mind foremost, are mind-made" ' (p. 28). Such a philosophy seems unfavorable to those whose use and control of the mind is weak. Furthermore, while race, colour, caste and social class is immaterial in respect of entry to the order of Buddhist *bhikkus* (holy men), 'entry is debarred to deformed persons, those suffering from such diseases as leprosy or tuberculosis . . .' (p. 84). Similar bans occur in ancient religious codes (e.g. those of the Hebrews) but seem incongruous to Western eyes when written in 1970.

In both Muslim and Hindu parts of Asia, the view is widespread that to attempt to rehabilitate the disabled person may be a form of defiance: a refusal to submit to the will of Allah, or an interference with the disabled person's *karma*. Westerners encountering such attitudes tend to deplore them heartily, in the clear self-assurance of superior knowledge. When a person's disability is redefined as her *culture*, as may happen in the case of communication disability, Westerners may be less eager to interfere.

Another view of karmic forces sees disability as:

'. . . not so simple as suffering for previous sins . . . one might need the experience of handicap in a particular incarnation for many reasons . . . not so much a punishment as what one needs for development at this particular stage. One might need perhaps to live with a certain kind of consciousness of the physical body, its limitations, its importance (or its unimportance); or to be made aware of the value of being helped by others, or (if a parent) giving help; or the need to live in love unfettered by intellect as with a Down's syndrome person . . . limitless possibilities'.

(Bayes, 1982)

Ambiguity of Attitude

It is often assumed that the rehabilitation game is uni-directional – disability being a universally undesirable condition which everyone tries to avoid or leave. However, self-disablement is also universal, e.g. by intoxication with various substances and with narcotic mass media, causing mental impairment and loss of mobility; by design and use of shoes that damage the feet, and clothing that deforms other parts of the body; by disuse of available lenses and hearing aids, or by use of darkened lenses, for cosmetic reasons; by chosen communication handicap and self-alienation through travel in countries where one does not understand the language.

The frequency of behaviour involving a known high risk of disablement, e.g. mountain sports, hunting, motor racing, also indicates an ambiguous attitude towards disability. Although the above disabilities and risks are initially temporary and controlled, the behaviour is often addictive. Some countries see deliberate mutilation for purposes of begging, or through local customs of sexual restriction or legal retribution.

Family Philosophy

The Asian family in rural areas and urban slums is largely free of the belief, found among a section of the European urban middle-classes, that the Government or society 'ought' to provide help with individual welfare problems, whether disabled children or elderly and frail persons, or substance abusers or sexual interference by mother on son. Such matters are the private concern of the Asian family. To expose private problems to the interested gaze of persons not closely related to one, and thus to become an object of pity, casual charity and bazaar gossip, would involve considerable loss of face.

The delinquent or impaired individual still belongs largely to the family

– he or she has few external rights or obligations. Society has few rights over her, or obligations towards him. The commonest form of State interference, i.e. obligatory schooling, impinges weakly. Most children pass through it, as through measles, with little permanent trace and with some acquired immunity. These realities, being in some contrast with those widely believed to exist in Europe, call into question most of the Western-inspired rehabilitation policies currently kicking around South West Asia.

Policies and Development

Government thinking about people with disabilities may pass through several identifiable stages, familiar to anyone who grapples with a new social welfare phenomenon (in whatever country):

(a)	*Ignorance*	The problem has yet to be perceived.
(b)	*Attention*	Ah! So there is a problem!
	Identification	What is it? Who are they?
	Differentiation	They are different! There is something wrong with them!
	Quantification	How many are there? How bad is it?
(c)	*Accommodation*	Something should be done about it!
	Segregation	There should be a place for them!
	Prevention	Can it be stopped?
	Economisation	How much is all this going to cost?
(d)	*Adaptation*	This thing must and can be managed!
	Conceptualisation	We have got to grips with the problem, exam-
	Specialisation	ined it, found some place for it and are getting familiar with it.
(e)	*Normalisation*	It is not so different or unusual.
	Integration	Maybe it can be managed in the normal health, welfare and educational provisions and facilities.
(f)	*Optionalisation*	This can be handled in many different ways,
	Individualisation	each with benefits and disadvantages. To provide several options gives the best chance of suiting individual needs.
(g)	*Reconceptualisation*	The whole thing can be seen in ways quite other than we first thought.

In practice, the above schema seldom progresses smoothly. After attention has been gained, and some basic quantification done, there may be a relapse into ignorance due, for example, to transfer of key personnel or switch of attention to a more pressing problem. Questions of cost and benefit recur, and may hasten the move towards, for example, integration as a cheap solution. Different members of key Government departments are likely at any one time to be thinking at different levels. The move from (c) where government officials accept that there is a problem needing attention and believe that there should be a solution, to (d) where practical steps are being taken to discover which solutions might actually work, may take many years.

Official thinking may undergo the fairly rational movement outlined above, but will also be influenced by practical experience – 'My old aunty became deaf, and we nearly went crazy shouting in her ear'. 'My nephew was in a road accident and is confined to a wheelchair. Main problem is that of toilet.' – and also of deep-rooted feelings – 'The deformed baby must be paying for its mother's sins; better not to touch such an issue.' 'I used to stammer at school, and the other children gave me hell. No child with a disability should ever be made to go through that torment.'

Western Advice

When a Government thinks it would like to do something, or has accepted an aid package including some cosmetic welfare items to lighten, for example, a rather gloomy deal of armaments, the Western Rehabilitation Advisor may enter the fray. She is often an experienced rehabilitation professional, capable of applying special educational or therapeutic techniques and training others to apply them, and possibly of managing an institution. She usually thinks about disability at levels (e) and (f). Her experience of how governments work in the West may be small; of how they work in Asia, usually nil (level a).

Western rehabilitation advisors have made proposals of many levels of improbability. For example, a scheme to send a task force of behaviourally trained female clinical psychologists to the villages of Nepal foundered on the fact that there was (then) only one psychologist in the country, a male of the species, and he was neither clinical nor behaviourally trained. A scheme at Peshawar, to fit intellectually advanced young deaf children with modern hearing aids, teach them expertly for several years with maximum parent-school cooperation, and then integrate them in normal schools 'to show what can be done', foundered on the unavailability of tests for the intellectual proficiency in deaf children of any age, and the fact that Urdu, the medium of school instruction, is the mother tongue of very few children in Peshawar.

Asian counterparts of Western advisors have mostly been too polite with this sort of useless proposal; or they have themselves had no better idea than the sort of top-down, fragmented, profession-dominated, gadget-bound scheme that has too often been foisted onto the third world by proselytisers for various dubious methodologies.

UN Alternatives

UN agencies advising Governments on rehabilitation development have basically been UNICEF, the World Health Organization, UNESCO, the International Labour Organisation, and UNCSDHA (UN Centre for Social Development and Humanitarian Affairs).

The *WHO* saw itself as the natural lead organisation, following the traditional medical domination of the disability field. Since 1976 it has engaged in the promotion of so-called 'Community Based Rehabilitation', with the idea of piggy-backing these services onto existing national primary health care schemes. Initially quite well-conceived, this approach deteriorated into a poorly-informed, inflexible package.[4] Well established primary health care 'piggies' are hard to find. Ten years after it began, India's senior rehabilitation planners commented that though the WHO scheme was still under trial in various countries, there was no report of any success (Narasimhan and Mukherjee, 1986).

The level of non-realism in the WHO scheme is indicated by some advice from the draft[5] fourth revision of the manual that is central to the scheme: 'When you play with the child you should have the child's whole attention . . . You will want to choose a quiet place where the child will think about playing with you. If there are people and noise where you are playing, he or she will want to look at what is happening. Then the child will not learn'. Intended to encourage family members and others to play with disabled children in the villages and slums of the third world, this lacks credibility.

UNICEF, with a global brief for children and women, focused initially on disability *prevention*, avoiding the need for difficult and expensive detection and intervention. But UNICEF has slowly understood that immunisation fails to interest people unless they see the link with disability avoided later. So it must tackle the visible problems of disability, or lack credibility in promoting prevention.

UNICEF's revised manual[5] of guidance on disability programs largely ignores the present and previous efforts of families, local traditional therapists and other community resources to assist and integrate their disabled members: 'less than 2 per cent receive rehabilitation services of any kind'. In the primary health field, educators eventually recognised useful indigenous practices and built on them, rather than treating rural and slum dwellers as ignorant and helpless. The rehabilitation field, twenty years on, is busy repeating the same top-down mistakes.

UNICEF has shirked a critical evaluation of the sparse results of the WHO-style rehabilitation, with its pointless antithesis between 'institution' and 'community' base. Trying to demystify rehabilitation, UNICEF risks belittling the skills of the few resource people in third world countries: 'They need to realise that rehabilitation techniques are no more mysterious or specialised than any others, and anyone can learn them'.

UNCSDHA, the agency intended to coordinate the Decade of Disabled People, has won little more than token cooperation from the other main agencies. It produced a 'World Programme of Action Concerning Disabled Persons' and a manual on the development of national disability plans (UNCSDHA, 1983b; 1986). Both are quite well written, but the obligatory jargon of 'full participation, integration and equalisation of opportunity' naturally has little impact on the minds of Asian officials thinking at levels (b), (c) or (d).

UNCSDHA wisely rejects a central antithesis of the WHO strategy: 'Rather than create an "either/or" dichotomy of developing highly specialised services in urban areas, or completely decentralised "community-based services" in the peripheral villages, intermediate solutions may be considered. One such solution would be to develop small-scale resource centres in the district towns, reaching out at a later stage to villages in the vicinity.' (UNCSDHA, 1986 p. 22)

UNESCO, occupied with internal conflicts in recent years, has used its small special education budget to publish more than forty books, case studies and other specialist papers, mostly outlining Western good practice in special education. Many are well-written and informative, though the sometimes poor quality of production and translation has reduced their impact.

One obscurely printed UNESCO Guide for teachers, parents and community workers (Baine, 1986) advocates construction of 'ecologically valid conceptual inventories' to determine a 'suitable curriculum for handicapped students', yet recommends North American textbooks for reading and maths, asserting of one that 'The skills taught in this textbook will generally be suitable in most cultures' (p. 30); and of the other, that 'The instructional procedures described would generally be suitable for any culture' (p. 31). So much for ecological validity.

The *International Labour Organisation* advises on vocational and social rehabilitation. The 'social' part is interpreted liberally, reaching down the age-range into early youth. UNICEF stretches its 0–5 age-group upwards, trying to meet the ILO and thus cover the gap left by UNESCO's budgetary eclipse. The ILO cultivates a more practical image than the other UN agencies, has produced several useful publications, and tries to promote information and awareness, for example through its BLINDOC service.

The major rehabilitation NGOs, (Non-Government Organisations)such as Rehabilitation International, the World Blind Union, the International League of Societies for Persons with Mental Handicap, and Disabled People's International, are naturally dominated by urban Westerners and their third world counterparts. They abound in goodwill and rhetoric, and have made commendable efforts to broaden their horizons, but have not yet achieved much understanding of the realities of rehabilitation planning in Asia. They have made little impact on official thinking.

Unfavorable Prognosis

Six years after IYDP, the Government of Pakistan recently announced its decision 'to build homes for the mentally retarded and mentally disturbed women. . . . Each home will have 25 to 50 inmates' (*The Pakistan Times*). Western advice (including our own) has failed to hit the button. The world economic climate, and Asian demographic realities, suggest that in the next decade there will be only token special provision for Asians with disabilities. A few more institutions will be provided, mostly of a sort that Western consultants abhor. In rural areas, where modern health care is marginally present, the 1990s will see practically no formal rehabilitation services. For most disabled people, the International Decade will pass without trace.

The number of disabled people will increase sharply. In Pakistan, the 2 million (2 per cent) with severe disabilities in 1988 will be 3 million by the year 2000. Including China, India and Bangladesh, the present 40 million with severe disabilities will be 52 million, on a conservative estimate, by 2000 AD.

Development Trends

The life-needs of millions of disabled Asians – a modest amount of food, shelter, company and hope – are supplied by their families, regardless of UN or government initiatives. Adaptations to a life with mild or severe disability are made, with more or less skill, by the people concerned. Information that might increase such skills is available in a few urban resource centres. Processing such information for mass media dissemination is technically quite feasible. No other current strategy could make an appreciable difference to the millions of disabled people remote from urban institutions.

Table 4 (Miles, 1988) indicates the strategy options. All five strategies outlined in the table are in fact 'information based' – but not all have been so conceived. All deal with the transfer of theoretical information and applied information (i.e. skills) between people. Possession of, and access to, the appropriate information has to a large extent dictated strategies.

In traditional rehabilitation, information has often been inadequate, unrecorded, informally acquired and very narrowly accessible. There has seldom been any intention of making it widely available. Institutionalised rehabilitation provides a more adequate level of information, formal recording, narrow transmission through professional training, some feedback and accountability, and narrow access. Client/family or community based rehabilitation tries to broaden transmission and access, with some loss of adequacy and accountability of information. The local rehabilitation resource centre approach is being tested in Pakistan and India to overcome this loss.

The respective strengths and weaknesses of these approaches have been analysed in detail by Serpell (1986). However, all four strategies have been implemented largely in ignorance of the background concept of *information*. The rehabilitation game requires reconceptualisation in terms of information, i.e. as *Information Based Rehabilitation*.

Information Based Rehabilitation

Information on disability, and on provisions for special education and rehabilitation, accumulates informally with disabled people, their families, and traditional healers. Information on providing formal services is available with many professionals, and in print and audio-visual material. Some rehabilitation skills and information grow informally in the community, for example, the family that develops a signing system with its deaf member; the local carpenter who makes exercise apparatus for spastic children; teachers who have several disabled pupils casually integrated; the schoolgirl who visits daily to read a chapter of a novel to a blind person.

Information *needs* are varied: the parents who have just learnt that their baby has a degenerative syndrome; the health visitor who wants to refer a child for optical examination; the girl who wants to know whether she

Table 4   Rehabilitation Development Strategies to 2000 AD

Designation	Key Features	Actors	Locations	Period
Traditional Rehabilitation	Narrow information base / Well adapted to local religion/ideology/economy / Often stigmatising	Local healers, holy persons, disabled persons	All localities at all times	
Institutionalised Rehabilitation	Methods, Gadgets, Labels, Buildings, Budgets	Professionals and 'cases'	Urban clinics, hospitals and special schools	1950s to 1980s
Client/Family or Community Based Rehabilitation	Consumer self-advocacy, self-help, integration, normalisation and demystification	DPs, Families, Skilled persons	Home, local community	1970s and 1980s
Resource Centre Based Rehabilitation	Middle way between institutionalized and community based rehabilitation / Giving away skills	Skilled persons, DPs and families	Local centres and homes	1980s and 1990s
Information Based Rehabilitation	*Theoretical Information* — Redefining roles and values / Restructuring language and thinking / Facilitating attitude change *Applied Information* — Replication of rehab skills / Mutual help, access and feedback / Freedom to choose among many options	All above actors and locations, plus mass media and information personnel, plus 'general public' (no longer differentiated by ability/disability or by skills status)		Made explicit from 1990s onwards

will have to care for her Down's syndrome brother when she is grown up; the teacher who has to visit a pupil paralysed after a fall in the gym; the wheelchair user who needs a ramp to enter a lecture hall; the manager who needs to know whether he can reasonably hire a job applicant with epilepsy.

In the past, meeting such demands required access to many sources. No society yet has a global plan for collecting and making available rehabilitation information, but such a plan is feasible if the field is reconceived *with information as the key variable*. Rehabilitation and special education methods and techniques are mostly communicable by print and audio-visual media, with sufficient intelligibility. These media can multiply and deliver information much more quickly and cheaply (though with less accuracy and control) than the medium of trained professionals located in specialised institutions.

Information systems are under study in Pakistan (Miles, 1987) to supplement the modest pool of rehabilitation skills, and to overcome the segmentation that drains the pool to mutually impermeable buckets. Several levels of information in Urdu on eight categories of disability, appropriate to four main categories of potential users, are targeted. Efforts are being made to fill gaps and publish appropriate information packages for each level and category of disability. Further targets will be set for audio-visual media. Accessible, accountable dissemination points are being identified, which will also monitor feedback, complete the information loop and establish on-going systems.

Theoretical information alone can hardly bring about rehabilitation. The necessary educational and therapeutic skills are in fact 'applied information', which may be consumed directly or via mediators, who may be teachers, social workers, family, consumer peers or, in the future, rehab-info technicians. Careful field-testing and adaptation is essential, to ensure accurate transfer of appropriate information and consequent empowerment of disabled people. Information *from* disabled persons *to* professionals may also facilitate necessary attitude changes. Monitoring and evaluating access, feedback and benefit requires flexible, action studies.

All-singing, all-dancing

Rural Asian health workers already carry a pocket sized medical reference library on microfiche with a lightweight reading device, giving them greater access to organised health information than was available to any doctor before 1950. The technology is already available, though not yet mass produced, for a lap-top, buffalo-proof, battery-operated, solar-rechargeable, limitedly interactive, rehabilitation library comprising, say, 5,000 illustrated pages, with assisted steering to access and screen-display required data.

This gives the potential to identify and assess a wide variety of disabilities and levels of severity in pre-electric villages, and to watch on screen, with relevant audience, commentated sequences of hands-on therapy with that type of disability. Call-in facility by satellite link will make available rapid reference to central advice. Rehabilitation technicians of the future will know first of all how to handle information equipment. For hands-on rehabilitation knowledge, they could train themselves on the job using their own 'three-dimensional' information resources – though this may never be officially sanctioned. In the village, if the technician makes her equipment work it will have sufficient credibility.

Getting It Together

The methods and technology described above are all in use now, but fragmented and uncoordinated because they have been seen merely as adjuncts to existing strategies rather than as the next major strategy in the pipeline.

The political leaders of mankind have so far not found compelling reasons to use advanced technology to spread appropriate health and rehabilitation information to the villages and slums of the third world. Like any other strategy, rehabilitation information needs to be *sold* to governments, professionals and the public with all necessary gimmicks, demonstrations, sex appeal and the whole sickening paraphernalia of modern marketing.

There is little doubt that Information Based Rehabilitation *can* be marketed. Major obstacles will be inertia and the vested interests of professionals and western disabled persons organisations, which may be threatened or upstaged by the entry of millions of third world disabled people into the reckoning.

Integrating Attitudes

The information-assisted local discovery of solutions to disability problems should in the long run have a positive effect on individual and community attitudes, which the impact of information technology in general may reinforce. At present the global 'desired' image of human beings used by advertising agencies invokes freedom and potency, which usually means being male, 30-ish, healthy, wealthy, light-brown skinned. Since more than 97 per cent of the human race are the 'wrong' sex, age, colour, health and bank status, there is room for substantial modification in the desired image.

Disability seems even less likely to develop a desirable global image than, for example, feminine gender, dark brown skin or old age. However, when cause, type, prognosis and management become more generally familiar it may be easier to separate and value the person who happens to have the disability, since the disability will have ceased to be the most significant part of her identity. Such revaluation may be unwelcome to the disabled person herself: some people seem to prefer a partial or minority identity by gender, skin-colour, disability, ethnicity, sexual orientation etc., rather than entering upon a broader identity as human.

How far does Information Based Rehabilitation need to be culturally translated to fit Asian lives and concepts? (Mass immunisation, for example, protects children against diseases even though 98 per cent of their parents have no idea how it works.) The extent to which rehabilitation information is adaptable and translatable is being studied in many countries. There is often high motivation among consumers to make their own adaptions, since appropriate outside information is the catalyst that will mobilise or redirect their own already-existing resources and energies.

To base rehabilitation on *information* and to plan for widespread dissemination will involve introducing physical therapists to medical anthropologists, sitting down special teachers with video script-writers, getting market researchers to rub noses with psychiatric social workers. This, of course, is already beginning to happen in the basic health education field, from which a great deal can be learnt.

In recent years, kalashnikovs and video game arcades have blossomed in Peshawar, between the buffalos and children's kites: where motivation is present and the means can be found, the millions in less-developed Asia update themselves very rapidly in technological sophistication. One benefit of Information Based Rehabilitation is that it involves a transfusion of new skills and people into a currently rather drab field. Communications media personnel tend to be future-oriented and open to new technology and a rapid pace of change. If such people are encouraged to play with new gadgets *and* feel that they are achieving morally praiseworthy ends, they may succeed in beaming the rehabilitation game into the twenty-first century.

Notes

1 South West Asia in this paper will be principally India, Pakistan and Bangladesh, which have a common history and administrative structure, though great diversity of language and culture. (UN agencies divide the region differently, e.g. Pakistan is in South East Asia for UNICEF, but in Eastern Mediterranean for WHO. Some agencies use 'South Middle Asia' for the old British India).

2 These figures are calculated by a conflation of data on India, Pakistan and Bangladesh from UN sources. They are intended to sketch trends, and may be regarded as approximations.

3 I have reviewed the scheme in detail elsewhere (Miles, 1985b).

4 The WHO and UNICEF manuals, while already in practical use in many countries, remain at the time of writing 'not formally published'.

References

Ahmadullah, M. *et al.* (1981) 'Situation of handicapped children in Bangladesh', *Assignment Children* 53/54, Geneva, UNICEF.

Baine, D. (1986) *Testing and Teaching Handicapped Children and Youth in Developing Countries*, Paris, UNESCO.

Bayes, K. (1982) Personal communication.

Directorate General of Special Education (1986) *Directory of special education programmes in Pakistan*, Islamabad, Government of Pakistan.

Gazi, S (1986) 'Disability and Rehabilitation in Bangladesh', Paper presented at the Eight Asia and Pacific Conference of Rehabilitation International, Bombay, September 1986.

Miles, M. (1983) *Attitudes towards persons with disabilities following IYDP (1981) With suggestions for promoting positive changes*, Peshawar, Mental Health Care.

Miles, M. (1985a) *Children with disabilities in ordinary schools: An action study of non-designed educational integration in Pakistan*, Peshawar, Mental Health Centre.

Miles, M. (1985b) *Where There Is No Rehab Plan*, Peshawar, Mental Health Centre.

Miles, M. (1987) 'Handicapped children in Pakistan: targeting information needs', *Health Policy & Planning*, 2, 4, pp. 347–351.

Miles, M. (1988) *Development Trends in Rehabilitation*, Peshawar, Mental Health Centre.

Narasimhan, M. and Mukherjee, A. (1986) *Disability: A Continuing Challenge*, New Delhi, Wiley Eastern.

Nimbkar, K. (1975) *Survey of Institutions for the Handicapped in India*, Bombay, Nimbkar Rehabilitation Trust.

Saddhatissa, H. (1970) *Buddhist Ethics – Essence of Buddhism*, London, George Allen Unwin, p. 28 and p. 84.

Serpell, R. (1986) 'Specialised centres and the local home community: children with disabilities need them both', *International Journal of Special Education*, 2, 2, pp. 107–127.

UNCSDHA (1983a) 'Activities at the National Level: Countries in the Asia and Pacific Region', *Disabled Persons Bulletin*, 3, pp. 21–38.

UNCSDHA (1983b) *World programme of action concerning disabled persons*, New York, United Nations.

UNCSDHA (1986) *Manual on Equalisation of Opportunities for Disabled Persons*, New York, United Nations.

Chapter Eight

'Inside We Are All Equal': A European Social Policy Survey of People Who Are Deaf

Lesley Jones and Gloria Pullen

'Deaf people should get together and tell governments about their situation. I would like the government to treat deaf people the same as hearing people. I do not like to see them thinking that to be deaf is also to be unintelligent. Inside we are all equal.

This is a quote from a Portuguese deaf man in Lisbon. He was telling us his opinion as part of an EEC project about deaf people in Europe. The project aimed to find out deaf people's opinions on social policy in Europe and to improve the situation by finding out what deaf people actually want themselves. The deaf people we interviewed were people whose preferred means of communication was sign language. It was an important project because of the way it was carried out as well as the content. It was the first to approach deaf people themselves in the sign language of their own country on an international level. The interviews were carried out in sign language by a deaf interviewer so it was direct deaf-to-deaf person interviewing. Previously work has been carried out by hearing people interviewing deaf people. There were communication problems for the deaf people with expressing their feelings and working through interpreters. There has been earlier work done by Jim Kyle and Gloria Pullen (1984) on young deaf people in employment using deaf researchers.

The project was funded by the European Economic Community's Bureau for Action for Disabled People. The money was channelled through the European Regional Secretariat of the World Federation of the Deaf, who initiated the work. It was administered through the Universities of Durham and Bristol. There were two researchers – Lesley Jones who is hearing and Gloria Pullen who is deaf. The method used is very innovative. People were contacted firstly through the deaf associations, then by sending a video of Gloria Pullen signing. It is important to use video and graphics rather than written material. One hundred deaf people were interviewed individually in five contrasting membership states in Spain, the Federal Republic of West Germany, Denmark, Portugal and Greece. The populations of these countries are as shown in Table 1.

Table 1

Country	Population
Germany	62 million
Spain	38 million
Denmark	5 million
Portugal	10 million
Greece	10 million

To provide a representative sample they were chosen because of size (as can be seen from the table) wealth (Denmark has the highest gross national product per head of population and Portugal the lowest), and provision for deaf people. We wanted a contrast of countries between those where the Government provides well developed services for deaf people and those where there are very limited services. As there was only a short time and a small budget only five countries were visited. Information was requested from the other countries in the EEC.

Group discussions were held in each country and the President of each deaf association was interviewed. A representative sample of twenty people were interviewed in each country. Ten of these were in a large city and the rest as a contrast in a small place. We relied very heavily on the co-operation of deaf people in the deaf associations of each country we visited.

We asked about three main areas:

(a) *Education and training* (mainly after 16 years of age) The main concerns were integration/segregation, interpreters and access to education and training.

(b) *Employment* This included interpreters at work, access to employment, environmental aids and job satisfaction. How did people find work and what were their future plans.

(c) *Health* This focused on communication with health workers, the use of interpreters, access to health, information (particularly about AIDS and childbirth) and to health care delivery.

Underlying all these issues were questions about interpreters.

(a) How were they found?

(b) Were they paid?

(c) Were they satisfactory to the clients?

(d) Was there any interpreter training scheme?

The information was collected in sign language on video and translated into the indigenous spoken language of each country.

In the first part of the project we travelled to five countries where we received a warm and hospitable response from all the associations of the deaf. Deaf people have worked very hard to help us in this project. It could not have been done without the help of the Presidents and the people who gave up their time to be interviewed. The hearing interpreters contributed a great deal as well in terms of time and effort. The system of interviewing takes time but it was very successful.

How did this relatively new technique of interviewing work? First of all there was training for the person in each country who was going to conduct the interviews. The interviews took place between two deaf people from the same country in the sign language of that country. The interviews were video-recorded with a sign language interpreter next to the camera speaking into a microphone (in the spoken language of that country). The researchers were there with the video watching the questions and keeping an eye on things, the hearing researcher keeping a low profile. Questions were asked about demographic details to the people outside waiting to come in. In the group discussions we had a half circle with the video. This was made possible as a group interview by people raising their hands when they wanted to speak so the others in the group knew who was next. The three topics of education, employment and health were then discussed. The resulting discussions were lively and interesting.

There was, throughout the project, a recognition of the significance of deaf people being able to express their opinions directly in their own language. The project worked through the deaf community and the materials used incorporated that culture as far as possible.

Deaf People's Lives

In this next section we will look at some of the things that deaf people said about their lives in Europe in the 1980's. The project was a qualitative piece of work. We were interested in how people saw their lives and their own perceptions of work, education and health. Let's look at the three topics in turn.

Education

A Greek woman in Athens talking of her experience said:

> At 16 I went to a high school with hearing people. I was all alone, the only deaf person there. I worked very hard, wrote and wrote, my teacher said 'Good, good'. She was a good teacher with a big heart. She helped me; she let me sit beside her. She showed me off to the hearing pupils and said 'Look how well she studies!' I got more strength from this, but in my heart I felt alone. I studied well but I was alone.

This woman takes us straight to the burning issue of education for people who are deaf: segregation or integration? This was one of the main topics that emerged from our interviews on the theme of education. There was a strongly expressed need for segregation from the people we interviewed in all five countries. The feeling of isolation described so well by the Greek woman was not unusual. It was almost as if there was a tide of integration sweeping over Europe amongst educationalists. Spain had just been swept along. Greek and Portugese theorists could only aspire to it as a future prospect. Germany was fully involved. Denmark, however, was beginning to espouse segregation again for children who were deaf, feeling that they had suffered because of integration policies. The deaf people there certainly felt this was so. We almost felt like saying to the countries who were looking to integration for the future 'Hang on, pour your money and resources into the services you have got in segregated schools, make them better. The tide is changing. By the time you have got integration, the tidal wave of educational fashion will have receded and you will be left stranded!' Bearing in mind the nature of the people we were interviewing – that they were committed to the use of sign language – this desire for segregated schooling is hardly surprising.

The use of sign language was important in the respondents' views of education. Very few people had been educated in their first language, sign language. Germany in particular had a very strong oral tradition. In Denmark there was a much greater readiness for children to be educated in sign language and although not officially recognised as a language as in Sweden, sign language had a much more formal role in education than in the other countries. Deaf people expressed the desire to learn in their own language.

Interpreters were seen as vital for access to tertiary education and train-ing but apart from in Denmark they were largely unavailable. (This project could have been called 'apart from in Denmark', as you will find that a familiar phrase by the end of the chapter!).

Denmark stood out in terms of educational provision. Ninety-five per cent of 60,000 interpreter hours in 1986 were for educational interpreting. Danish school-leavers who are deaf are entitled to interpreter support for two years further education or training. They also receive financial support to pay the interpreters.

Teachers who were deaf themselves looked like being a part of the future in deaf education. Denmark had deaf teachers and so, surprisingly, did Greece (only four). Older German deaf people spoke of having had deaf teachers when they were children but mainly in woodwork or craft subjects. Interestingly, a Greek respondent who became a teacher talks about her own career pattern in a way which shows this is not always an intentional strategy on the part of authorities:

> I applied to the government with my papers. It doesn't say any-where that I am deaf. The government accept my application. I started work and afterwards they discovered I was deaf. They were amazed.

However, we met several deaf people both training and working as teach-ers of the deaf in Denmark and Greece. It was seen as important that deaf children saw deaf adults who could provide them with good role models. One of the authors remembers thinking she would grow up to be hearing as all the adults at her school were hearing.

There were criticisms about teacher training. These centred on the generalised training for teaching 'the disabled' rather than specialising in working with people who were deaf. There were requests for specific input both on deafness and communication skills. There were still deaf people being taught by teachers who had no idea how to communicate with them.

There was marked frustration amongst deaf people about the lack of opportunity to follow study and training courses. There was a lack of access to courses which would lead to better job prospects. There was also a strong vocational bias to the opportunities that were offered.

Deaf people wanted there to be an adult educational provision for hearing parents of deaf children about deafness and communication skills. More contact with deaf adults for hearing parents was another suggestion for an education programme, giving them a much clearer idea of the capabilities and achievements of people who are deaf.

Apart from in Denmark, some few deaf people were still missing out an education completely or not going to school until later. We had to change the question 'When did you leave school?' as a way of finding out how much schooling people received. We soon realised that leaving school at 21 meant very little if you did not begin school until 14 years of age.

One Portuguese woman in a rural area had only been sent to school at 11 when her mother had taken her to the nearest town when she was going to the dentist and he had told her that there were schools for children 'like that'.

Deaf people reported learning material that they did not understand and leaving school inadequately prepared to earn a living. They also told of repeating the year's work two or three times when there were not enough deaf children who were up to the standard to go on to the next stage.

There was a strong feeling that deaf people should be consulted and be more involved in education of the deaf. This was only true of Denmark up until now.

Training

The training section of the interviews revealed an informal training network amongst deaf people. People seeking work would sometimes find work alongside other deaf employees and they would provide the necessary training. This was true of industries such as leatherwork, printing, tailoring and baking where there were a number of deaf people working together.

Written selection tests limited access for deaf people to training courses for work because of their lack of education in written and spoken language. Tests, such as dictation tests, obviously worked against them and little attempt had been made, in any of the countries visited to adapt these tests.

There was marked frustration at the lack of possibilities for training for work, particularly outside the sometimes limited vocational training given in schools for deaf children. This training included areas such as tailoring, printing, leatherwork, joinery and baking.

Adult education of a more general nature, such as evening classes done for leisure and advancement, was also mentioned and was something which was denied to most people who were deaf. Tutors did not know how to communicate with their deaf students and it was difficult to follow the class unless a hearing member of the group agreed to help with notes of the lectures. Interpreters, apart from in Denmark, were difficult to obtain for adult education courses. Interestingly, all the countries, particularly Spain and Denmark, had adult education courses run by deaf tutors for deaf people.

Employment

A young Spanish draughtsman talking about employment prospects for deaf people describe it in the following way:

> Deaf people cannot reach the same level as hearing people. We'll never advance, education does not prepare us so we cannot get good jobs. We only get jobs which allow us to feed ourselves, but no more than that.

This brings us neatly to the main point about employment and people who are deaf within these five countries. The major problem did not seem to be one of unemployment (although this was beginning to emerge) but of *under-employment* and thwarted ambition. People were finding work in jobs which they felt were less than they were capable of doing. There was an expectation that they should be grateful to have a job, rather than a feeling that they could choose to develop and progress in their careers.

Under-employment was partly related to the occupational segregation for deaf people which clearly existed in all five countries. There was a concentration of deaf people in certain jobs. As previously mentioned, carpentry, printing, leather work, baking, tailoring and dressmaking are still seen as 'suitable' work for people who are deaf. Employers found it 'easier' to employ a group of deaf people together in these areas at work. Schools still encouraged training in these areas, perhaps related to the demands of the labour market? The two things are obviously inter-related. Rather like the nineteenth century British education system for the 'working classes', with its concentration on domestic service for girls and physical work for boys, education for deaf children still seems to be geared to low expectations of achievement and finding a place in the labour market. A Portuguese man described this under-employment very well:

> Here in Portugal most of the deaf people work as carpenters, blacksmiths or doing menial work. They are not civil servants or working in banks. The Ministry of Employment does not support deaf people really.

The system for finding work was only formalised in Denmark (and then only in Copenhagen) where there was an adviser for deaf people seeking work. Mostly deaf people relied on family and friends, other deaf people or the staff from the schools for the deaf. As mentioned before, there was an informal 'deaf apprenticeship' scheme and this was an extension of a network for finding employment through other deaf people.

Communication with hearing people at work emerged (not surprisingly) as a problematic area inhibiting promotion. Examples were given of some hearing people learning basic sign language usually when working closely with a group of deaf people. But employers rarely knew anything about how to communicate with their deaf employees.

The quota system seemed to be unsuccessful for deaf people seeking work. There was a strong feeling that deaf people lost out to people with other disabilities because of the written and dictated selection tests which were felt to discriminate against people who were deaf.

Environmental aids at work were virtually unknown outside Denmark. Fire alarms were not visual ones so deaf workers had to rely on hearing collegues to alert them, otherwise, as one German worker said 'we'd all barbecue!'. The expense of installing environmental aids clearly discouraged employers from doing so and possibly from taking on workers who were deaf.

There seemed to be a future prospect for co-operatives. Spain had a co-operative of deaf workers based on a government subsidy. The Danish deaf people talked of co-operatives as an option linked to the deaf association itself.

There was a strong need for interpreters for training for work, seeking work and in the work place. The importance of work in the European deaf people's lives is well illustrated by the following quote from a Danish woman:

> It is important to have a good job. If you have a boring job it's as
> if you aren't worth anything.

The relationship between work and self-esteem is neatly described in this quote and for people who are deaf it is especially important in societies that do not particularly value their members who have a disability.

Health

A German printer talking about his experience of having a hernia operation said:

> The doctor gave me an anaesthetic; I became anxious during the
> operation because the doctor took something out of the marrow
> of my spine with a large needle. I couldn't understand what he said
> because he was wearing a mask. I was alarmed. What were they
> looking for in my spine? It was a hernia operation for goodness
> sake! Eventually he calmed me down. I asked him afterwards what
> was happening. The doctor explained that it was an anaesthetic.

This man was describing being given an epidural anaesthetic with an explanation which was incomprehensible to him. He could not lip-read a doctor wearing a mask over his mouth. The procedure has a risk of paralysis and the increased stress caused by the lack of communication for both patient and doctor was not only unpleasant but potentially hazardous. This situation summarises the problems caused by communication difficulties in a health care setting. Unless an interpreter is used, communication can sometimes become impossible.

Treatment may become more frightening and therefore more painful because of the lack of explanation about what is happening. Research has shown that procedures that are not explained are perceived as more painful by patients.

Family and friends were the most commonly used interpreters, apart from in Denmark where health service interpreters were available. Letters sent out for hospital appointments were accompanied by information about interpreters.

Family and friends were not, however, always perceived as the best interpreters by the deaf people using them. There was a lack of confidentiality experienced by the deaf people. They also felt that sometimes their relatives and friends gave poor explanations of treatment and diagnoses because of their lack of understanding of the technical terms used. Misunderstandings in this situation can lead to incorrect compliance with drug treatment regimes and can be dangerous. A doctor mumbling 'three times a day' whilst looking down at a prescription pad is unlikely to be understood.

The other aspect of health is that, apart from the delivery of health care itself, where people who are deaf seem to receive a less full service, they are also denied access to most health information. The use of the written and spoken word as the main medium of communication denies them access to health promotion material of the most wide-reaching type, such as preparation for childbirth, AIDS and smoking education. Reliance on the written word is ineffectual when many deaf children leave school with only a very limited ability to read. Even the AIDS campaign had failed to reach some of our respondents. One man in Portugal said, 'I've been very careful about what I eat since I heard about AIDS.'

People who were deaf also complained of the lack of confidence that the doctor understood what they were complaining about in the first place. Decisions or diagnosis may be wrong when taking a history if the doctor cannot understand his patient. The *right to be understood* is a very important one alongside the *right to understand*.

The point was also made that for deaf people, there was no possibility of going to get help in the wider field of health care, such as Women's Aid or Helplines like the Samaritans, in the same way that hearing people could. This point was made in Denmark but not in countries such as Portugal and Greece, where they were still struggling to obtain basic human rights in health care. There interpreters were virtually impossible to obtain. It is important though that counselling and support services are extended to include deaf people. In the future, following Denmark's approach, there was hope expressed for direct access to deaf counsellors and deaf professionals. Having a third person there, an interpreter, was not felt to be ideal in matters of emotional problems. Text telephones were also not felt to be appropriate for counselling.

Deaf people wanted most of all to have more interpreters, properly trained, to work in the health service. It was felt that health workers needed communication training and deaf awareness courses.

Conclusion

The project gave a deaf perspective on social policy. People who are deaf have been virtually excluded from the decision making process about their own lives. This project gave information about the ways in which that could be changed.

The method of video-recording in the indigenous sign language of each country showed that cross-cultural comparisons can be made. The quality of information is high from having directly deaf to deaf person interviews. The use of graphics and video material is vital when working with people whose main means of communication is sign language. This project did successfully obtain qualitative material on deaf people's lives. The influences of race, gender and social class are obviously important too in a complex relationship with deafness, but the perceptions of everyday life provide a valuable view of how changes can be made.

The support of national deaf associations was vital. Deaf and hearing researchers can work together in a useful collaboration, provided that the rules of both deaf and hearing cultures are adhered to.

To summarise what European deaf people wanted, it is clear that independence and the recognition of sign language were the major aims. Interpreters were an important part of this goal in education, health and employment. In order for deaf people to gain qualifications, work and equal access to services, interpreters were invaluable. There was a need for interpreter training and financial support. Denmark clearly emerged as having the best service provision for deaf people; as a richer, smaller country and with a more equitable political philosophy than the other countries this was inevitable. However, their model is a good one to look at. Denmark provides subsidised text telephones for all people who are deaf. (There is unfortunately no standard European system making telephone communication difficult for deaf people between countries). Denmark also provided free videos for deaf people and a country wide free video service. These two things give vital access to information for people who are deaf. Combined with an efficient interpreter service, they make it much more possible for deaf people to have equal access to services. In Greece, Portugal and Spain, however, and to a lesser extent the Federal Republic of West Germany, they were still fighting for more basic human rights. However, a great deal had been achieved by the deaf associations. We have mentioned the Danish deaf associations. The Spanish Deaf Association had a wide-ranging cultural programme of activities and had produced historical and literary material in graphics and video in order to improve knowledge and the poor educational achievement of people who are deaf. Portugal and Greece, both with little financial support, were providing adult education with deaf tutors and trying hard to provide better educational facilities. The German Deaf Association had fought for free transport concessions for its members. Sign language was stressed throughout as of vital significance. Recognition of deaf people as a linguistic minority rather than a 'disabled group' seemed to be the overall trend in terms of gaining equality of opportunity. The certainty of being recognised as a group with different needs was seen as crucial. Demanding recognition of rights as a minority group with its own culture and language seemed to be the way that the deaf associations were moving. Working together through the European Regional Secretariat of the World Federation of the Deaf was obviously giving strength to this argument.

Notes on Contributors

Paul Abberley is a disabled sociologist working at Bristol Polytechnic, teaching mainly on Health and Social Work courses.

Len Barton is Head of Department (Academic and Professional Development) in the Department of Education at Bristol Polytechnic. He is chairperson of the *British Journal of Sociology of Education* and editor of the international journal *Disability, Handicap and Society*. He is particularly interested in the politics and social aspects of disability.

Robert Burgess is Professor of Sociology and Director of CEDAR (Centre for Educational Development, Appraisal and Research) at the University of Warwick.

Marion Blythman is Head of the Department of Professional and Curriculum Support Studies at Moray House College, Edinburgh.
Since 1984 she has also worked as an educational consultant to the HCHC project, described in the 6/75 chapter. She describes this as 'the greatest learning experience of my life, i.e. living in New York and working in some of the toughest areas of a very tough city'

Mano Candappa is Research Fellow in Sociology at the University of Warwick.

Bob Hudson is a Senior Lecturer in Social Policy at New College, Durham, where he has been teaching since 1970. His main interest is in the field of the personal social services. He has written widely on many aspects of this, particularly in *Community Care* and *The Health Service Journal*, as well as contributing to academic quarterlies.

Lesley Jones is a Hearing Research Fellow at the Department of Sociology and Social Policy, University of Durham (she is currently based in the Research Unit, School of Education, University of Bristol). She is co-author of *Words Apart: Losing your Hearing as an Adult*, (Tavistock, 1987).

M. Miles works at the Mental Health Centre, Mission Hospital, Peshawar, NWFP, Pakistan and has written extensively on issues of Rehabilitation and the Third World.

Mike Oliver is a Reader in Disability Studies at Thames Polytechnic, having previously worked as a Lecturer at the University of Kent and as a Development Officer for Kent Social Services. He is the author of numerous articles on disability and the book *Social Work with Disabled People* (MacMillan, 1983), and is actively involved in the disability movement, currently serving on the Executive and Management Committee of the Spinal Injuries Association.

Gloria Pullen is a Deaf Research Assistant in the Department of Sociology and Policy, University of Durham and the Research Unit, School of Education, University of Bristol.

Frieda Spivack is an Associate Professor at Herbert H. Lehman College, City University of New York and is Research Director and founder of Hospital/Clinic, Home/Centre Instructional Programs Corporation (HCHC), which is mainly situated at Kingsbrook Jewish Medical Centre and at three other sites in Central Brooklyn, New York City.

Wolf Wolfensberger, now a Professor at Syracuse University in upstate New York, was one of the early promoters of community service systems and normalization. He is the designer of citizen advocacy, and of the PASS and PASSING evaluation tools.

Index

voucher system 50

Wagner Report on Residential Care
    (1988) 50
welfare 3, 30, 38, 57–8, 66
    appeals 51
    Asia 113
    cost 17, 85
    hotels (New York) 89, 98, 102
    legislation 107
    officers 37
    recipients 64, 67

USA 2, 30, 42–3, 53, 85–7, 90, 107
    vouchers 50
welfare state restructuring 8–9, 12, 17–21
wheelchairs 16, 73, 78, 116, 122
    Het Dorp 37
    housing 65
    training for social workers 61
women's movement 60, 62
    see also feminism
World Blind Union 119
World Federation of the Deaf 127, 137
World Health Organization 117, 118,
    125

.

Printed in the United States
by Baker & Taylor Publisher Services